Christmas with Southern Living 2008

Oxmoor House

©2008 by Oxmoor House, Inc.
Book Division of Southern Progress Corporation
P. O. Box 2262, Birmingham, Alabama 35201-2262

Southern Living® is a federally registered trademark belonging to
Southern Living, Inc.

ISBN-13: 978-0-8487-3228-8
ISBN-10: 0-8487-3228-6
ISSN: 0747-7791
Printed in the United States of America
First Printing 2008

Oxmoor House, Inc.
Editor in Chief: Nancy Fitzpatrick Wyatt
Executive Editor: Susan Carlisle Payne
Art Director: Keith McPherson
Managing Editor: Allison Long Lowery

Christmas with Southern Living® *2008*
Editor: Rebecca Brennan
Foods Editor: Julie Gunter
Project Editor: Terri Laschober Robertson
Copy Chief: L. Amanda Owens
Copy Editor: Donna Baldone
Editorial Assistant: Vanessa Rusch Thomas
Director, Test Kitchens: Elizabeth Tyler Austin
Assistant Director, Test Kitchens: Julie Christopher
Test Kitchens Professionals: Jane Chambliss; Patricia Michaud;
   Kathleen Royal Phillips; Catherine Crowell Steele;
   Ashley T. Strickland; Kate Wheeler, R.D.
Photography Director: Jim Bathie
Senior Photo Stylist: Kay E. Clarke
Associate Photo Stylist: Katherine Eckert
Director of Production: Laura Lockhart
Senior Production Manager: Greg A. Amason

Contributors
Designer: Amy Heise Murphree
Indexer: Mary Ann Laurens
Copy Editor: Catherine C. Fowler
Editorial Assistant: Cory L. Bordonaro
Interns: Rebekah Flowers, Erin Loudy
Photographers: Robbie Caponetto, Beau Gustafson, Lee Harrelson
Photo Stylists: Melanie J. Clarke, Missy Crawford, Kappi Hamilton,
   Leslie Simpson, Katie Stoddard

To order additional publications, call 1-800-765-6400.

For more books to enrich your life, visit **oxmoorhouse.com**

To search, savor, and share thousands of recipes, visit **myrecipes.com**

Cover: Two Herb-Roasted Turkey with Bourbon Gravy (page 12)
Back Cover: (*clockwise from top left*) Honey-Roasted Grape
   Tomato Crostini (page 109); Classic Colors (page 92);
   Garden-Fresh Greetings (page 62); Gingerbread Girls (page 131)

Contents

SET THE MOOD, SET THE TABLE, BAKE THE GOODIES, AND ENJOY!

This book belongs to:

....

CHRISTMAS 2008

Christmas with Southern Living 2008

Oxmoor House

THESE PAGES OFFER INSPIRATION FOR EVERY DETAIL OF THE HOLIDAY SEASON.

WITH THESE COMPLETE MENUS AND TABLE-SETTING IDEAS,
YOU AND YOUR GUESTS WILL HAVE PLENTY TO CELEBRATE.

Entertaining

CHRISTMAS *Family Gathering*

This bountiful menu delivers great flavor and evokes nostalgia for a simpler time.
Pass these hearty dishes around the table family-style for some old-fashioned togetherness.

menu

Two Herb-Roasted Turkey with Bourbon Gravy

Country Ham and Sage Dressing

Cranberry Chutney (page 35)

Roasted Brussels Sprout Salad

Roasted Apples and Sweet Potatoes in
Honey-Bourbon Glaze

Old-Fashioned Green Beans

Creamed Cauliflower with Farmhouse Cheddar

Dinner rolls

Coconut Cake

serves 12

Set a Unique Place

Usher your family and friends to the holiday table with these ultra cute, miniature chalkboard trugs (shallow wooden gardening baskets) as place cards. Clip variegated holly, pine, Leyland cypress, and pepper berry to fill each trug. No floral foam or water is needed; these materials will stay fresh for several days. Write names on chalkboard strips. (See Where to Find It on page 170 for trugs.)

2 weeks ahead:
- Make grocery list. Shop for nonperishables.
- Plan table centerpiece and/or decorations.

3 or 4 days ahead:
- Finish remaining shopping.
- Place turkey in refrigerator to thaw, if frozen.

2 days ahead:
- Make cake layers, wrap in plastic wrap, and refrigerate.
- Cook cauliflower, transfer to zip-top plastic bag; chill.
- Bake sweet potatoes; cool and chill.

1 day ahead:
- Make frosting, assemble cake, cover loosely with plastic wrap, and chill.
- Prepare dressing, and spoon into a baking dish; cover and chill, unbaked, overnight.
- Make sauce for cauliflower, assemble dish, cover and chill.
- Make dressing for Brussels sprout salad.
- Prepare and chill Cranberry Chutney (page 35).

5 hours ahead:
- Assemble and bake Roasted Apples and Sweet Potatoes.

4 hours ahead:
- Prepare turkey; bake. Cover with aluminum foil.

2 hours ahead:
- Cook giblets and neck for Bourbon Gravy.
- Roast Brussels sprouts.
- Let dressing come to room temperature.
- Let cauliflower casserole come to room temperature.
- Simmer green beans with bacon.

1½ hours ahead:
- Assemble Brussels sprout salad (don't add dressing).
- Bake cauliflower casserole.
- Bake Country Ham and Sage Dressing.

45 minutes ahead:
- Reheat Roasted Apples and Sweet Potatoes.
- Finish making Bourbon Gravy.
- Bake dinner rolls.
- Take cake out of refrigerator.

10 minutes ahead:
- Dress Brussels sprout salad.

Two Herb-Roasted Turkey with Bourbon Gravy

This tender and juicy bird is prepared with a traditional technique and has classic flavor. A bourbon-splashed gravy makes it extra-special. Be sure to set aside half of the gravy for the kids before adding bourbon.

Prep: 23 min.   Cook: 3 hr.   Other: 15 min.

1	(12- to 14-lb.) fresh or frozen turkey, thawed
6	Tbsp. unsalted butter, softened
1½	Tbsp. minced fresh sage or 1½ tsp. rubbed sage
1½	Tbsp. fresh thyme leaves or 1½ tsp. dried thyme
2	tsp. salt
1	tsp. pepper
1	large onion, cut into wedges
2	celery ribs, coarsely chopped
3	garlic cloves, halved

Garnishes: fresh sage and fresh flat-leaf parsley
Bourbon Gravy

Remove giblets and neck from turkey; place in refrigerator for use in gravy, if desired. Rinse turkey with cold water; pat dry with paper towels. Place turkey, breast side up, on a rack in a lightly greased roasting pan. Lift wing tips up and over back, and tuck under bird.

Combine butter and next 4 ingredients in a small bowl; rub 2 Tbsp. seasoned butter inside turkey cavity. Place onion, celery, and garlic inside turkey cavity. Rub remaining 4 Tbsp. seasoned butter all over outside of turkey, legs and all. Tie ends of legs together with heavy string, or tuck under flap of skin around tail.

Bake, uncovered, at 325° for 2½ to 3 hours or until a meat thermometer inserted into the meaty part of thigh registers 170°. Shield turkey with aluminum foil towards end of cooking, if necessary, to prevent overbrowning.

Transfer turkey to a serving platter, reserving pan drippings for Bourbon Gravy. Let turkey stand, covered with foil, at least 15 minutes before carving. Garnish platter, if desired. Serve turkey with Bourbon Gravy.
Yield: 12 to 14 servings.

editor's favorite

Bourbon Gravy:

Prep: 5 min.   Cook: 1 hr., 8 min.

Giblets and neck reserved from turkey
Pan drippings from turkey
½   cup all-purpose flour
½   tsp. garlic powder
2   Tbsp. bourbon

Combine giblets, neck, and 3 cups water in a saucepan. Bring to a boil; cover, reduce heat, and simmer 45 minutes to 1 hour or until giblets are tender. Strain, reserving broth. Discard turkey neck. Coarsely chop giblets; set aside.

Add reserved broth (2 cups) to turkey pan drippings; stir until browned bits are loosened from bottom of roasting pan.

Transfer broth and drippings to a saucepan, if desired, or continue cooking in roasting pan placed over 2 burners on the stovetop. Stir in chopped giblets, if desired. Bring to a boil; reduce heat, and simmer, uncovered, 3 to 5 minutes.

Combine flour and ½ cup water, stirring until blended; gradually stir into gravy. Bring to a boil; boil 1 minute or until thickened. Set aside some plain gravy, if desired. Stir garlic powder and bourbon into remaining gravy. Serve hot. **Yield: about 3 cups.**

Fix It Faster: Substitute canned chicken broth instead of making homemade broth, if desired.

Country Ham and Sage Dressing

This dressing is good any time of year. Serve it alongside roast chicken or pork.

Prep: 25 min. Cook: 1 hr., 13 min.

1	(1½-lb.) loaf firm-textured white bread, cut into ¾" cubes
½	cup unsalted butter, divided
½	lb. country ham, cubed
2	medium onions, chopped (about 4 cups)
4	celery ribs, chopped (about 2 cups)
6	garlic cloves, minced
2	cups chicken broth
1	large egg, beaten
1	tsp. pepper
⅔	cup chopped fresh flat-leaf parsley
3	Tbsp. minced fresh sage
1	Tbsp. minced fresh thyme

Spread bread cubes in a single layer on 2 large baking sheets. Bake at 350° for 10 minutes or until toasted. Let cool, and transfer to a very large bowl.

Melt 1 Tbsp. butter in a large deep skillet over medium-high heat; add country ham, and sauté 2 to 3 minutes. Add ham to bread in bowl.

Melt remaining butter in same skillet over medium heat; add onion and celery, and sauté 8 minutes. Add garlic, and sauté 2 minutes. Remove from heat; add to bread in bowl. Combine broth, egg, and pepper. Add broth mixture to bread, tossing well. Stir in fresh herbs. Spoon dressing into a lightly greased 13" x 9" baking dish.

Bake, covered, at 400° for 30 minutes. Uncover and bake 15 to 20 more minutes or until top is browned and crusty. **Yield: 12 servings.**

Make Ahead: Prepare dressing a day ahead. Store dressing, unbaked, in refrigerator. The next day, let dressing stand at room temperature 30 minutes and bake as directed. Reheat briefly just before serving.

Roasted Brussels Sprout Salad

This vibrant holiday salad can be served warm or even made ahead and served at room temperature.

Prep: 20 min. Cook: 30 min.

1	Tbsp. Dijon mustard
1	large garlic clove, finely minced
2	to 3 Tbsp. white wine vinegar
½	tsp. sugar
½	tsp. salt
¼	tsp. pepper
½	cup olive oil
3	lb. Brussels sprouts
⅓	cup olive oil
1	tsp. salt
½	tsp. pepper
2	cups grape or cherry tomatoes, halved
⅔	cup minced green onions
¼	cup minced fresh flat-leaf parsley

Whisk together first 6 ingredients; gradually whisk in ½ cup oil until blended. Set aside.

Rinse Brussels sprouts thoroughly, and remove any discolored leaves. Trim stem ends; cut in half lengthwise. Combine Brussels sprouts and next 3 ingredients in a large bowl; toss to coat. Transfer Brussels sprouts to 1 or 2 large rimmed baking sheets, spreading into 1 layer.

Roast at 450° for 25 to 30 minutes or until tender and browned, stirring once. Transfer roasted Brussels sprouts to a serving bowl, and cool slightly. Add tomatoes, green onions, and parsley; toss to blend. Add desired amount of dressing, and toss to coat. Serve warm or at room temperature. **Yield: 12 to 16 servings.**

Roasted Apples and Sweet Potatoes in Honey-Bourbon Glaze

Prep: 32 min.   Cook: 1 hr., 47 min.   Other: 45 min.

5	large sweet potatoes (about 5 lb.)
3	Golden Delicious apples
¼	cup fresh lemon juice
⅔	cup firmly packed brown sugar
½	cup honey
6	Tbsp. unsalted butter
¼	cup bourbon
1	tsp. ground cinnamon
½	tsp. ground ginger
½	tsp. salt
⅔	cup coarsely chopped pecans

Wash sweet potatoes, and place on a baking sheet; prick with a fork. Bake at 400° for 1 hour or until almost tender. Remove from oven. Let stand 45 minutes or until cooled.

Meanwhile, peel and core apples. Slice apples into ⅓" thick wedges; toss with lemon juice in a bowl.

Peel cooled potatoes, and slice ⅓" thick. Arrange potatoes and apples alternately in a greased 13" x 9" baking dish. Pour remaining lemon juice over potatoes and apples.

Combine brown sugar and next 6 ingredients in a saucepan, stirring well. Bring to a boil over medium heat, stirring occasionally; boil 2 minutes or until slightly thickened. Pour glaze over potatoes and apples. Bake, uncovered, at 400° for 30 minutes.

Remove from oven; baste with glaze in bottom of dish, and sprinkle nuts across top. Bake 14 to 15 more minutes or until apples look roasted. Baste with glaze just before serving. **Yield: 12 servings.**

Old-Fashioned Green Beans

These beans are simmered long and slow with premium double-smoked bacon to develop that trademark "Southern-style" goodness. Red pepper flakes add a nice punch to the dish.

Prep: 12 min.   Cook: 1 hr.

½	lb. double-smoked bacon, diced*
1	medium onion, chopped
3	lb. green beans, trimmed
1	tsp. dried crushed red pepper
1	tsp. salt
2	Tbsp. unsalted butter, softened
2	to 3 Tbsp. cider vinegar

Roasted Apples and Sweet Potatoes in Honey-Bourbon Glaze

Cook bacon in a Dutch oven over medium heat 10 minutes or until browned and crisp. Add onion, and sauté 5 minutes or until tender. Stir in green beans, red pepper, and salt. Add enough water to cover green beans. Bring to a boil; cover, reduce heat, and simmer 40 to 45 minutes or until beans are very tender. Drain beans, and transfer to a bowl. Add butter and vinegar; toss well. Serve hot. **Yield: 12 servings.**

*We discovered 2 great online sources for the specialty bacon: Schaller and Weber from www.germandeli.com and www.nodinesmokehouse.com. Regular bacon is an option too but contributes a milder flavor.

Creamed Cauliflower with Farmhouse Cheddar

Prep: 12 min.   Cook: 58 min.

2	large heads cauliflower (about 2½ lb. each), cut into florets
3	Tbsp. unsalted butter
½	cup minced green onions
2	large garlic cloves, minced
3	Tbsp. all-purpose flour
2	cups milk
2	cups heavy whipping cream
½	tsp. salt
½	tsp. freshly grated nutmeg
¼	tsp. black pepper
¼	tsp. ground red pepper
1	cup (4 oz.) shredded Farmhouse Cheddar cheese or sharp Cheddar cheese
1½	cups fresh breadcrumbs*
¼	cup freshly grated Parmesan cheese
½	tsp. salt
¼	tsp. pepper
3	Tbsp. unsalted butter, melted

Bring 4 qt. salted water to a boil in a large Dutch oven over high heat. Add cauliflower; cook just until crisp-tender, stirring often. Drain; rinse under cold water. Let cool in colander.

Melt 3 Tbsp. butter in a large skillet over medium heat; add green onions and garlic, and sauté 3 minutes. Whisk in flour until smooth. Cook 1 minute, whisking constantly. Gradually whisk in milk and cream; cook over medium heat, whisking constantly, until mixture is thickened and bubbly. Stir in ½ tsp. each salt and nutmeg and ¼ tsp. each pepper. Add cheese, stirring until cheese melts. Remove from heat; add cauliflower, stirring to coat well. Spoon cauliflower into a greased 13" x 9" baking dish.

Combine breadcrumbs and next 3 ingredients in a small bowl; sprinkle over cauliflower. Drizzle with melted butter. Bake, uncovered, at 400° for 35 minutes or until browned and bubbly. **Yield: 12 to 14 servings.**

*To make 1½ cups homemade breadcrumbs, place 3 slices bread, torn, in a mini chopper. Cover and pulse just until you have fine crumbs.

Note: Farmhouse Cheddar gets its distinction, in part, because it's made on a farmer's property, using only milk from his cows. We tested with Keen's.

Coconut Cake

Prep: 10 min.   Cook: 25 min.   Other: 5 min.

1¼	cups unsalted butter, softened
1½	cups sugar
4	large eggs
3	cups all-purpose flour
2	tsp. baking powder
½	tsp. salt
1	cup coconut milk
1	tsp. vanilla extract
1	tsp. coconut extract

Coconutty-Pecan Frosting

Grease 2 (9") round cake pans with shortening, line pans with wax paper, and grease paper. Dust with flour, shaking out excess.

Beat butter at low speed with an electric mixer 2 minutes or until creamy. Gradually add sugar, beating at medium speed 5 minutes or until light and fluffy. Add eggs, 1 at a time, beating just until yellow disappears.

Combine flour, baking powder, and salt in a medium bowl. With mixer at low speed, add dry ingredients alternately with coconut milk, beginning and ending with dry ingredients. Add extracts. Pour batter into prepared pans.

Bake at 350° for 23 to 25 minutes or until a wooden skewer inserted in center comes out clean. Cool layers in pans on wire racks 5 minutes; remove from pans, and cool completely on wire racks. Cake layers can be wrapped and chilled up to 2 days, if desired.

Spread Coconutty-Pecan Frosting between layers and on top of cake; let ooze down sides. **Yield: 1 (2-layer) cake.**

Coconutty-Pecan Frosting:

Prep: 5 min.   Cook: 10 min.

1	(12-oz.) can evaporated milk
1½	cups sugar
¾	cup butter
4	egg yolks, lightly beaten
2½	cups unsweetened organic coconut flakes
1½	cups chopped pecans
2	tsp. vanilla extract

Combine milk, sugar, butter, and egg yolks in a 3-qt. heavy saucepan. Bring to a simmer over medium heat; cook 8 to 10 minutes or until frosting is thickened, stirring occasionally. Remove from heat. Stir in coconut, pecans, and vanilla. Let cool. **Yield: 4¼ cups.**

Coconut Cake

FARMHOUSE *Holiday Breakfast*

A hearty country breakfast in front of a crackling fire is a dream come true on any winter morning. Farm-fresh eggs enhanced with herbs, sugar-smoked bacon, fluffy biscuits, and homestyle charm are the highlights of this meal.

menu

Farmers Market Scramble

Smoky Brown Sugar Bacon

Puffy Cheese Grits

Jalapeño Biscuits   Spiced Honey Butter

Streusel-Spiced Coffee Cake

Cider-Glazed Christmas Fruit

Steaming Hot Mocha

Orange juice   Milk

serves 12

Put All Your Eggs in This Basket

If you have the good fortune of access to farm fresh eggs—your own or from a local farm—make them your centerpiece theme. Pile eggs in a wire basket and surround them with rag balls, apples, and oranges. Tuck in sprigs of fresh greenery to complete the scene. (For rag balls, see Where to Find It on page 170.)

game plan

2 weeks ahead:
- Make grocery list. Shop for nonperishables.
- Plan table centerpiece and/or decorations.

2 days ahead:
- Do remaining shopping.
- Prepare Spiced Honey Butter; cover and refrigerate.

1 day ahead:
- Mix together coffee cake; cover and refrigerate unbaked.
- Prepare Cider-Glazed Christmas Fruit; cover and refrigerate.
- Measure out sugar and cocoa for Steaming Hot Mocha.

2 hours ahead:
- Prepare and bake bacon. Cool completely; cover loosely at room temperature.
- Bake coffee cake.
- Prepare and cut biscuit dough; place on baking sheet.

1 hour ahead:
- Prepare Steaming Hot Mocha; cover and keep hot until ready to serve.

40 minutes ahead:
- Prepare and bake cheese grits.
- Gather ingredients for scrambled eggs.

20 minutes ahead:
- Bake biscuits.
- Scramble eggs.
- Reheat Cider-Glazed Christmas Fruit.

*For recipe at right, we used 1½ (1-lb.) packages Nueske's applewood smoked bacon to yield the 24 slices; otherwise, any thick-cut bacon, smoked or not, would also work fine in this recipe.

quick & easy

Farmers Market Scramble

Hearty scrambled eggs get a punch of flavor with fresh herbs and tomato.

Prep: 10 min.   Cook: 14 min.

24	large eggs
½	cup milk
¼	cup whipping cream
1½	tsp. salt
½	tsp. freshly ground pepper
½	tsp. hot sauce
¼	cup butter, divided
1	large tomato, chopped and drained on a paper towel
⅓	cup chopped fresh chives
¼	cup chopped fresh flat-leaf parsley

Whisk together first 6 ingredients in a large bowl.

Melt 2 Tbsp. butter in a large nonstick skillet over medium heat; add half of egg mixture, and cook, without stirring, until eggs begin to set on bottom. Draw a spatula across bottom of skillet to form large curds. Cook until eggs are thickened but still moist. (Do not stir constantly.) Stir in half of tomato. Remove from heat, and transfer to a warm platter. Repeat procedure with remaining butter, egg mixture, and tomato. Sprinkle whole platter of eggs with chives and parsley; serve hot. **Yield: 12 servings.**

editor's favorite

Smoky Brown Sugar Bacon

This bacon takes a little while to prepare, but it's more than worth it. The aroma alone gets our highest rating.

Prep: 12 min.   Cook: 20 min. per batch

3	cups firmly packed light brown sugar
24	slices applewood smoked bacon (we tested with Nueske's)*

Spread brown sugar onto a large plate; dredge half of bacon in sugar, pressing to be sure plenty of sugar sticks to both sides of bacon. Place bacon in a single layer on a large baking rack on an aluminum foil-lined rimmed baking sheet. Bake at 425° for 18 to 20 minutes or until crisp. Remove bacon from rack to a serving platter or parchment paper to cool. Repeat with remaining bacon and brown sugar. **Yield: 24 slices.**

Puffy Cheese Grits

This airy grits casserole stands tall as it finishes baking. Plan to bring it straight from the oven to the table.

Prep: 21 min.   Cook: 20 min.

1	cup milk
1	cup water
1	tsp. salt
1	cup uncooked quick-cooking grits
⅓	cup unsalted butter
¼	tsp. ground white pepper
4	large egg yolks
1½	cups (6 oz.) shredded Monterey Jack cheese
8	large egg whites
¼	tsp. cream of tartar

Combine first 3 ingredients in a large saucepan. Bring to a boil; stir in grits. Reduce heat, and simmer 3 minutes or until thickened, stirring often. Remove from heat; add butter and pepper, stirring until butter melts. Stir in egg yolks, 1 at a time, and cheese.

Beat egg whites and cream of tartar at high speed with an electric mixer until stiff peaks form. Fold one-third of beaten egg whites into grits; carefully fold in remaining egg whites. Pour into a lightly greased 13" x 9" baking dish. Bake at 425° for 20 minutes or until puffed and browned. Serve immediately. **Yield: 12 servings.**

Round out this menu's farmhouse theme by serving milk in old-fashioned, single-serving milk bottles.

Jalapeño Biscuits

If you prefer less heat in these big yummy biscuits, seed the jalapeños before chopping them.

Prep: 15 min. Cook: 18 min.

4   cups all-purpose flour
2   Tbsp. baking powder
1   tsp. salt
⅔   cup butter, chilled and cut into pieces
2   medium jalapeño peppers, minced (about ¼ cup)
1½ to 1¾ cups buttermilk
Melted butter (optional)

Combine first 3 ingredients; cut in ⅔ cup butter with a pastry blender or 2 knives until crumbly. Stir in jalapeño. Add buttermilk, stirring just until dry ingredients are moistened.

Turn out dough onto a lightly floured surface, and knead lightly 3 or 4 times. Pat or roll dough to ½" thickness; cut with a 2½" round cutter. Place on a lightly greased baking sheet.

Bake at 425° for 16 to 18 minutes or until golden. Brush with melted butter, if desired, before serving. **Yield: 20 biscuits.**

make ahead • quick & easy
Spiced Honey Butter

Make this sweet and spicy butter in advance so the flavors have a chance to blend; it's wonderful spread over coffee cake or fresh-from-the-oven biscuits.

Prep: 9 min.

1   cup unsalted butter, softened
¼   cup raw honey or regular processed honey
¼   tsp. freshly grated nutmeg
¼   tsp. ground cinnamon
Pinch of ground cloves

Combine all ingredients in a bowl; beat at medium speed with a handheld electric mixer until blended. Serve at room temperature. Store in refrigerator. **Yield: 1¼ cups.**

make ahead
Streusel-Spiced Coffee Cake

Prep: 16 min. Cook: 35 min. Other: 8 hr.

¾   cup unsalted butter, softened
1   cup granulated sugar
2   large eggs
1   cup sour cream
2   cups all-purpose flour
2   tsp. baking powder
1   tsp. baking soda
½   tsp. ground cinnamon
½   tsp. grated nutmeg
½   tsp. salt
¾   cup firmly packed light brown sugar
1   cup coarsely chopped pecans
½   tsp. ground cinnamon
¼ to ½ tsp. grated nutmeg

Beat butter at medium speed with an electric mixer until fluffy; gradually add granulated sugar, beating well. Add eggs, 1 at a time, beating until blended after each addition. Add sour cream, mixing well.

Combine flour and next 5 ingredients; add to butter mixture, beating well. Spread batter into a greased and floured 13" x 9" pan.

Combine brown sugar, pecans, ½ tsp. cinnamon, and ¼ to ½ tsp. nutmeg in a small bowl. Sprinkle evenly over batter. Cover and refrigerate 8 hours.

Uncover; bake at 350° for 35 minutes or until a wooden pick inserted in center comes out clean. **Yield: 12 servings.**

Cider-Glazed Christmas Fruit

An apple cider reduction and two kinds of apples create layers of flavor in this buttery glazed fruit that is equally good served over waffles, pancakes, or ice cream.

Prep: 7 min. Cook: 25 min.

1   cup apple cider
6   Tbsp. unsalted butter, divided
¾   tsp. ground cinnamon
1   Tbsp. brown sugar
3   Granny Smith apples, peeled, cored, and sliced
3   Braeburn apples, unpeeled, if desired, cored, and sliced
½   cup granulated sugar
2   cups fresh cranberries

Pour apple cider into a medium skillet. Cook over medium-high heat 14 minutes or until syrupy. Remove from heat, and stir in 2 Tbsp. butter and cinnamon. Set aside.

Melt remaining ¼ cup butter in a large deep skillet over medium-high heat. Stir in brown sugar. Add apple slices, tossing to coat. Sprinkle apples with granulated sugar, and cook, stirring often, 8 minutes or until apples are mostly tender. Transfer apples to a serving bowl using a slotted spoon.

Add cranberries to buttery drippings in skillet. Cook, stirring constantly, 2 minutes or until cranberries begin to pop. Stir in apple cider reduction, and cook 1 minute. Pour cranberry mixture over apples in serving bowl, and fold in gently. Serve warm. **Yield: 6 cups.**

Make Ahead: You can prepare Cider-Glazed Christmas Fruit up to 1 day ahead. Cover and refrigerate; reheat in microwave until warm.

quick & easy
Steaming Hot Mocha

Coffee combines with hot chocolate for a bracing drink to be enjoyed on the coldest of mornings.

Prep: 4 min.   Cook: 20 min.

2	cups sugar
1½	cups unsweetened cocoa
¼	tsp. salt
7	cups milk
7	cups strong brewed coffee
1	Tbsp. vanilla extract

Marshmallow crème (optional)

Combine first 3 ingredients in a Dutch oven. Whisk in milk and coffee until smooth. Cook mixture over medium heat, stirring often, 20 minutes or just until bubbles appear (do not boil); remove from heat. Stir in vanilla. Top each serving with marshmallow crème, if desired. **Yield: 15½ cups.**

Steaming Hot Mocha and Streusel-Spiced Coffee Cake

LIGHT & EASY *Company Brunch*

Who could ask for more than this luscious meal sparkling with color, fresh flavors, and healthy, wholesome goodness all on the same holiday table?

Basil Mary

menu

☙

Basil Mary

Bacon, Tomato, and Egg Gratin

Herb Buttermilk Biscuits

Griddled Grits with Cilantro Oil

Spinach Salad with Cornbread Croutons

Fruit Salad with Lemon-Mint Syrup

Coffee   Juice

serves 16

Beverage Bar
Plan ahead to have an assortment of refreshing drinks available for a brunch crowd of 16. Here's what we recommend:
• Coffee: Brew one large pot; transfer it to a thermal carafe. Brew a second pot. Set out creamer and sugar options.
• Juice: Buy a (64-oz.) container each of cranberry-apple juice and orange juice. Pour each into a carafe and nestle into a tub of ice.

Each recipe in this menu is accompanied by a nutrient analysis, so you can boast healthy entertaining.

game plan

2 days ahead:

• Set frozen O'Brien potatoes in the refrigerator to thaw. (It takes more than one day.)

1 day ahead:

• Make grits; cool and cut into triangles. Stack triangles on aluminum foil and seal edges of foil. Refrigerate.

• Make Cilantro Oil for grits; cover and refrigerate.

• Make custard for Bacon, Tomato, and Egg Gratin. Store in refrigerator.

• Make syrup for Fresh Fruit Salad with Lemon-Mint Syrup; cool. Chop mango slices and place them and the cooled syrup back in the bottle the mango came in. Refrigerate.

• Make cornbread croutons; cool and store in a zip-top plastic bag.

The morning of:

• Roast tomatoes; assemble and bake Bacon, Tomato, and Egg Gratin.

• Cut up fruit for salad. Combine fruit and syrup in a serving bowl; cover and chill.

• Place spinach in salad spinner to keep fresh. Slice onions, and store in a zip-top plastic bag in the refrigerator. Measure out cranberries and bacon, and store in another zip-top plastic bag in the refrigerator.

• Prepare Basil Mary.

30 minutes before guests arrive:

• Prepare and bake biscuits; remove biscuits from oven. Reduce oven heat to 300°. Add gratin to oven, and bake for 20 minutes to reheat. Turn off oven; keep gratin in oven and return biscuits to oven to keep warm.

• Cook grits triangles; reheat Cilantro Oil in microwave. Place grits on ovenproof serving platter; drizzle with oil. Cover with foil, and keep warm in oven.

• Assemble spinach salad. Add salad dressing just before serving, or serve on the side.

• Arrange gratin, fruit salad, and spinach salad on buffet. Add warm biscuits and grits as guests arrive.

---

quick & easy

Basil Mary

You'll love the fresh basil flavor in this classic cocktail. We liked it without vodka, but if you prefer a spirited version, add 3 cups chilled vodka to the pitcher before serving.

Prep: 14 min.

8	cups low-sodium tomato juice
1	cup packed fresh basil leaves
$\frac{1}{2}$	cup fresh lemon juice
$\frac{1}{4}$	cup Worcestershire sauce
1	Tbsp. hot sauce
$\frac{1}{2}$	to 1 tsp. freshly ground black pepper
$\frac{1}{4}$	tsp. celery seeds

Garnish: fresh basil

Place 1 cup tomato juice and 1 cup basil in a blender, and pulse until basil is pureed. Add lemon juice and next 4 ingredients. Add remaining tomato juice as needed to fill blender, and pulse to blend. Pour mixture into a serving pitcher; stir in remaining tomato juice.

Fill glasses half-full with crushed ice. Pour drink to fill glasses. Garnish, if desired. **Yield: 16 ($\frac{1}{2}$-cup) servings.**

Per serving (without vodka): Calories 31 (1% from fat); Fat 0g (sat 0g, mono 0g, poly 0g); Protein 1.1g; Carb 6.7g; Fiber 0.7g; Chol 0mg; Iron 0.7mg; Sodium 133mg; Calc 20mg

Bacon, Tomato, and Egg Gratin

Look for O'Brien potatoes (diced potatoes with onions and peppers) in the freezer section of the supermarket.

Prep: 5 min.   Cook: 1 hr., 5 min.

2	pints grape tomatoes
1	(28-oz.) bag frozen O'Brien potatoes, thawed (we tested with Ore-Ida)
$\frac{1}{4}$	cup chopped fresh chives
12	large eggs
2	tsp. coarse-grained Country Dijon mustard
1	tsp. salt
$\frac{1}{4}$	tsp. freshly ground pepper
1	(16-oz.) carton egg substitute
$\frac{1}{2}$	cup 1% low-fat milk
8	fully cooked bacon slices, chopped
$\frac{1}{4}$	cup shredded Parmesan cheese

Place tomatoes on a lightly greased rimmed baking sheet. Roast at 400° for 20 minutes or until tomatoes collapse and begin to brown.

Place potatoes in a lightly greased 13" x 9" baking dish. Sprinkle with roasted tomatoes and chives; toss gently.

Combine 1 egg, mustard, salt, and pepper in a large bowl; whisk until blended. Add remaining 11 eggs, egg substitute, and milk; whisk until blended. Pour over potatoes in dish. Sprinkle with bacon and Parmesan.

Bake, uncovered, at 350° for 45 minutes or until set. **Yield: 16 servings.**

Per serving: Calories 151 (40% from fat); Fat 6.7g (sat 2.1g, mono 2.4g, poly 1.2g); Protein 11.4g; Carb 11.2g; Fiber 1.4g; Chol 164mg; Iron 2mg; Sodium 379mg; Calc 71mg

Herb Buttermilk Biscuits

Sometimes known as "angel biscuits," this type of biscuit is made with yeast, which makes the end result extra light and tender. You can find fresh poultry herbs (a mixture of thyme, sage, rosemary, and marjoram) packaged together in many produce sections along with other fresh herbs. Otherwise, blend your own herbs as desired.

Prep: 17 min.   Cook: 15 min.   Other: 1 hr.

1	(¼-oz.) package active dry yeast
½	cup warm water (100° to 110°)
4½	cups all-purpose flour
½	cup yellow cornmeal
¼	cup sugar
1	tsp. baking powder
1	tsp. baking soda
1	tsp. salt
9	Tbsp. butter, divided
2	cups low-fat buttermilk
¼	cup finely chopped fresh poultry herbs

Butter-flavored cooking spray

Combine yeast and warm water (100° to 110°) in a 1-cup glass measuring cup; let stand 5 minutes.

Whisk together flour and next 5 ingredients in a large bowl. Cut 1 stick of butter into small pieces. Cut into flour mixture with a pastry blender until mixture resembles coarse meal. Add yeast mixture, buttermilk, and herbs; stir with a fork just until dry ingredients are moistened. Cover and chill dough for 1 hour.

Turn out dough onto a floured surface; knead lightly 5 times. Roll dough to ½" thickness; cut with a 2½" round biscuit cutter. Place biscuits on 2 large baking sheets

coated with cooking spray. Melt remaining 1 Tbsp. butter; brush lightly over biscuits.

Bake at 450° for 12 to 15 minutes or until golden. **Yield: 20 biscuits.**

Per biscuit: Calories 188 (28% from fat); Fat 5.8g (sat 3.4g, mono 1.4g, poly 0.4g); Protein 4.4g; Carb 29.3g; Fiber 1.2g; Chol 15mg; Iron 1.7mg; Sodium 267mg; Calc 51mg

Griddled Grits with Cilantro Oil

Prep: 12 min.   Cook: 26 min.   Other: 2 hr.

1	(14-oz.) can less-sodium, fat-free chicken broth
2	cups uncooked quick-cooking grits
1	tsp. salt
½	tsp. freshly ground black pepper
2	oz. fontina cheese, diced

Butter-flavored cooking spray

2	thin green onions, cut into 1" pieces
½	cup packed fresh cilantro leaves
½	cup canola oil
2	tsp. sherry vinegar or white wine vinegar

Bring 4 cups water and broth to a boil in a 4-qt. saucepan. Stir in grits, salt, and pepper. Bring to a boil, and cook, uncovered, 8 minutes or until very thick. Add cheese, stirring until it melts. Remove from heat, and pour grits into a 13" x 9" pan coated with cooking spray. Set aside to cool completely.

While grits cool, process green onions and cilantro in a small food processor until minced. With processor running, slowly add oil, and process until well blended. Pour cilantro oil into a small saucepan; set aside.

Cut cooled grits into 8 rectangles. Cut each rectangle into 2 triangles. Place a 12" cast-iron skillet over medium-high heat until hot; coat skillet with cooking spray. Add half of grits rectangles to skillet, taking care to keep rectangles together for easier turning. Cook 3 minutes; coat tops with cooking spray; turn and cook on other side 3 minutes or until golden. Transfer grits to a serving platter, separating rectangles into triangles, and keep warm. Repeat procedure with remaining grits rectangles.

Heat oil mixture over medium heat just until warm. Remove from heat, and stir in vinegar. Drizzle 1 tsp. oil evenly over each triangle; serve with remaining oil, if desired. **Yield: 16 servings.**

Per 1 grits triangle and 1 tsp. oil: Calories 120 (38% from fat); Fat 5.1g (sat 1g, mono 2.6g, poly 1.3g); Protein 2.8g; Carb 15.7g; Fiber 0.3g; Chol 4mg; Iron 0.8mg; Sodium 224mg; Calc 22mg

Make Ahead: Cut cooled grits as directed above. Cover and store in refrigerator. Brown grits and prepare herb oil just before serving.

Spinach Salad with Cornbread Croutons

This salad is simple to assemble and sports the holiday color of cranberries.

Prep: 5 min.   Cook: 6 min.

3	(6-oz.) packages fresh baby spinach, thoroughly washed
1	cup thinly sliced red onion (about 1 medium)
1	cup dried cranberries
½	cup fat-free red wine vinaigrette (we tested with Girard's)
8	fully cooked bacon slices, crumbled

Cornbread Croutons

Combine first 3 ingredients in a salad bowl. Add vinaigrette, and toss to coat. Sprinkle with bacon and Cornbread Croutons before serving. **Yield: 16 servings.**

Per serving: Calories 130 (25% from fat); Fat 3.7g (sat 1g, mono 1.8g, poly 0.5g); Protein 3.6g; Carb 21.9g; Fiber 3g; Chol 17mg; Iron 1.6mg; Sodium 398mg; Calc 41mg

Cornbread Croutons:

Prepare croutons up to a day ahead, and store them in a zip-top plastic bag until ready to serve.

Prep: 11 min.   Cook: 10 min.   Other: 1 hr., 4 min.

1	(8½-oz.) package corn muffin mix (we tested with Jiffy)
1	large egg
⅓	cup 1% low-fat milk

Stir together all ingredients in a bowl just until moistened; let stand 4 minutes. Using a spatula, spread corn **muffin batter into an 8" x 9" rectangle in a lightly greased, parchment paper-lined jelly-roll pan.**

Bake at 400° for 10 minutes or until golden; turn oven off, and remove cornbread. Cool. Cut cornbread into 1" cubes. Return cornbread to warm (turned-off) oven. Let stand in oven, with door closed, 1 hour or until croutons are dry and crunchy. **Yield: 5 cups croutons.**

Per ¼ cup: Calories 56 (29% from fat); Fat 1.8g (sat 0.5g, mono 0.9g, poly 0.2g); Protein 1.3g; Carb 8.6g; Fiber 0.8g; Chol 11mg; Iron 0.4mg; Sodium 139mg; Calc 13mg

Fruit Salad with Lemon-Mint Syrup

Prep: 27 min.   Cook: 2 min.

1   (24-oz.) jar sliced mangos in light syrup
1   large lemon
5   fresh mint leaves, crushed
4   large kiwifruit, peeled, halved lengthwise, and sliced
3   cups seedless red grapes
1   cup seedless green grapes
1   pomegranate, seeds removed and reserved
Garnish: fresh mint

Drain mangos, reserving 1 cup syrup. Peel 3 strips of lemon rind with a vegetable peeler; juice lemon to measure 3 Tbsp. Combine reserved syrup, lemon rind, lemon juice, and crushed mint leaves in a small microwave-safe bowl. Cover and microwave at HIGH 2 minutes or until syrup begins to bubble. Cover and cool completely; chill.

Cut mango slices into cubes, and place in a large bowl; add kiwifruit, grapes, and pomegranate seeds. Remove lemon rind and mint from syrup with a slotted spoon. Pour syrup over fruit; toss. Cover and chill until ready to serve. Garnish, if desired. **Yield: 16 servings.**

Per ½ cup: Calories 78 (2% from fat); Fat 0.2g (sat 0g, mono 0g, poly 0.1g); Protein 0.8g; Carb 20.5g; Fiber 1.5g; Chol 0mg; Iron 0.4mg; Sodium 3mg; Calc 16mg

Make Ahead: Prepare the syrup up to 1 day ahead, and refrigerate it until ready to assemble the salad.

A QUICK & EASY *Christmas Dinner*

When it comes to the big Christmas meal, timing is everything: Follow our step-by-step game plan and kitchen tips to host the most relaxed and enjoyable holiday possible.

menu

Poinsettia Sipper

Pimiento Cheese Pinwheels

Sliced Pears with Rémoulade Dollop

Sweet Apple and Mustard-Glazed Turkey

Cranberry Chutney

Moist Cornbread Dressing with Spicy Crawfish

Candied Yams

Wilted Collards with Bacon and Onion

Bread Pudding with Rum Sauce   or

Pumpkin Pie Ice Cream Fantasy

serves 12

game plan

1 week ahead:
- Assemble serving pieces; label what goes with what.

3 days ahead:
- Grocery shop.
- Make Cranberry Chutney. Put into serving dish; cover and refrigerate.
- Tear bread for bread pudding. Seal bread in zip-top plastic bag.

1 day ahead:
- Chill juices for Poinsettia Sipper.
- Prep lettuce for salad.
- Prepare collards; transfer to a foil pan, cover, and refrigerate. Refrigerate reserved bacon separately.
- Assemble Candied Yams; cover and refrigerate.

3 to 4 hours before guests arrive:
- Roast turkey, adding glaze near the end.
- Prepare and bake bread pudding.

1 to 2 hours before meal:
- Assemble pinwheels; place on baking sheet. Bake when oven is free.
- Prep pears for salad.
- Make Rum Sauce.

30 minutes before guests arrive:
- Stir together Poinsettia Sipper.
- Assemble pear salad; cover with plastic wrap.
- Reheat greens in oven. Add reserved bacon after reheating and prior to serving.
- Bake Candied Yams.
- Prepare dressing.
- Carve turkey.
- Freeze baked pie for 1 hour.

When guests arrive:
- Serve Poinsettia Sipper.
- Put salads on the table.
- Allow the guests who want to help you...help you.
- Have helper put hot food into designated serving dishes.
- Warm up Bread Pudding and Rum Sauce.

After dinner:
- Assemble Pumpkin Pie Ice Cream Fantasy.

---

quick & easy
Poinsettia Sipper

Mix this nonalcoholic aperitif right before serving.

Prep: 8 min.

1   (64-oz.) bottle 100% cranberry juice, chilled
1   cup thawed orange juice concentrate
1   (1-liter) bottle lemon-lime soft drink, chilled
1   lime, thinly sliced
½   cup fresh cranberries

Stir together first 3 ingredients in a large pitcher; garnish with lime slices and cranberries. **Yield: 16½ cups.**

---

quick & easy
Pimiento Cheese Pinwheels

Here's an easy appetizer recipe to help occupy the kids (pressing out dough and rolling it into logs) on a buzzing holiday.

Prep: 10 min.   Cook: 10 min.

2   (8-oz.) packages reduced-fat refrigerated crescent rolls (we tested with Pillsbury)
1   cup pimiento cheese*

Unroll crescent rolls on a lightly floured surface, and pat into 2 rectangles; press perforations to seal. Spread ½ cup pimiento cheese onto each rectangle, spreading to edges. Roll up each dough rectangle, starting at 1 long end; cut each into 10 even slices. Place pinwheels on a lightly greased baking sheet. Bake at 400° for 10 minutes or until browned. **Yield: 20 appetizers.**

*Use your favorite brand of pimiento cheese, your own recipe, or the widely available 5-oz. jars of sharp process cheese spread (Old English).

Easy Table Ideas

Here are three ideas for impressive and easy-to-create table decorations. Each can be made ahead.

Gift Box Centerpiece

Select a small empty box that will serve as the centerpiece. Set a jar or small vase on top of box; trace diameter of jar or vase onto center of box, and cut hole in box to match size. Wrap box. Add ribbon using double-sided tape or hot glue. Set the jar or vase filled with flowers, berries, and greenery into box hole. (Another really quick idea is to just place a small potted plant into the hole of the wrapped box.)

Mum Balls

To make 6 mum balls, buy 3 bunches of Kermit mums. Buy 6 oasis balls (about 5" to 6" in diameter). Soak oasis in water. Trim mums, leaving 1½" of stems. Stick mums into oasis, covering oasis completely. Spritz them periodically with water, and they should last up to 5 days.

Candy Cane Easels

For each easel, hot glue 2 candy canes together side by side (as if making an easel). Break a third candy cane halfway down the stem; hot glue it in place to serve as the back of the easel. Display holiday menu or place card on each easel.

Sliced Pears with Rémoulade Dollop

Sliced Pears with Rémoulade Dollop

Rémoulade is a classic French sauce often served with seafood, but we love it spooned over ripe pears in this salad.

Prep: 21 min.

6	firm ripe red pears, sliced
1	cup orange juice
12	Bibb lettuce leaves
¾	cup rémoulade dressing (we tested with Louisiana)
1	cup crumbled blue cheese
1	cup chopped pecans or pecan pieces

Combine pears and orange juice in a bowl.

Place lettuce leaves on salad plates. Remove pear slices from bowl with a slotted spoon, pat dry, and arrange over lettuce. Spoon dressing over pears. Sprinkle cheese and pecans over each salad. **Yield: 12 servings.**

Fix It Faster: For an easier salad, use fresh or canned pear halves and spoon dressing and toppings in center of each.

Sweet Apple and Mustard-Glazed Turkey

This year at Christmas, if convenience is key, try a ready-to-cook turkey and apply our simple glaze for dazzling results. You'll love the convenience of the oven-ready bird. Otherwise, you can buy a fresh or frozen turkey and visit www.myrecipes.com for basic prep and roasting instructions.

Prep: 4 min.   Cook: 3 hr., 45 min.

1	(12-lb.) ready-to-cook frozen turkey (we tested with Jennie-O)
1	(18-oz.) jar apple jelly
2	Tbsp. yellow mustard

Follow package directions carefully for baking turkey (while still frozen), allowing last 30 minutes of baking for adding glaze. (A 12-lb. frozen turkey should take 3½ to 4 hours to reach 170° in the breast.)

Combine jelly and mustard in a small saucepan, stirring well. Bring glaze mixture to a boil; boil 1 minute or until jelly is melted. Remove from heat. Set aside 1 cup glaze for serving.

When ready to apply glaze to turkey, carefully cut open top of oven bag, watching out for hot steam and juices. Pull bag away from top of turkey. Brush remaining ⅔ cup glaze over turkey in 2 additions during last 30 minutes of baking. Serve turkey with reserved 1 cup glaze. **Yield: 12 servings.**

Cranberry Chutney

Prepare this dressed-up cranberry sauce up to 3 days ahead, and chill it.

Prep: 5 min.

2	(16-oz.) cans whole-berry cranberry sauce
2	Tbsp. mango chutney (we tested with Major Grey)
2	tsp. orange liqueur (we tested with Grand Marnier)

Combine all ingredients in a bowl; stir well. Serve chilled or at room temperature. **Yield: 3½ cups.**

Moist Cornbread Dressing with Spicy Crawfish

To best enjoy this moist, quick stovetop dressing, make it just before sitting down to the big meal. Find frozen crawfish tails in the seafood department of some larger grocery stores or in local seafood markets. We recommend using crawfish tails harvested in the United States.

Prep: 6 min.   Cook: 10 min.

¾	cup butter, divided
¾	cup chopped onion
¾	cup chopped celery
2½	cups chicken broth
1	(16-oz.) package frozen cooked peeled crawfish tails, thawed and drained
¼	to ½ tsp. ground red pepper
1	(16-oz.) package seasoned cornbread stuffing (we tested with Pepperidge Farm)

Melt ½ cup butter in a large deep skillet or Dutch oven. Sauté onion and celery 4 to 5 minutes or until crisp-tender. Add chicken broth, crawfish tails, remaining ¼ cup butter, and red pepper; bring to a boil. Remove from heat. Add cornbread stuffing; gently toss and fluff with a fork until stuffing is moistened. **Yield: 12 servings.**

Candied Yams

High heat caramelizes these yams. The s'more-like topping is optional, but kids will love it.

Prep: 6 min.   Cook: 25 min.   Other: 10 min.

3   (40-oz.) or 4 (29-oz.) cans cut yams, well drained
     (we tested with Sugary Sam sweet potatoes in syrup)
1   cup firmly packed light brown sugar
¼   cup butter, melted
1   Tbsp. vanilla extract or vanilla bean paste
1   tsp. ground cinnamon
12   large marshmallows (optional)

Arrange yams in a lightly greased 13" x 9" baking dish. Sprinkle brown sugar over yams. Combine butter and next 2 ingredients. Drizzle over yams. Bake, uncovered, at 425° for 20 minutes. Sprinkle marshmallows over yams, if desired, and bake 5 more minutes. Let stand 10 minutes before serving. **Yield: 8 to 12 servings.**

make ahead
Wilted Collards with Bacon and Onion

Prepare these greens a day ahead, and reheat before serving. Don't stir in the crisp bacon until ready to serve.

Prep: 10 min.   Cook: 38 min.

5   thick bacon slices, chopped
2   cups chopped onion
½   cup chopped celery
1   Tbsp. bottled minced garlic
1   (14-oz.) can chicken broth
3   (16-oz.) packages frozen chopped collard greens
2   tsp. seasoned salt
½   tsp. black pepper

Cook bacon in a Dutch oven over medium-high heat 8 to 10 minutes or until crisp; remove bacon, and drain on paper towels, reserving drippings in pan. Set bacon aside.

Sauté onion and celery in hot drippings until crisp-tender. Add garlic, chicken broth, and remaining ingredients. Cover and cook over low heat 25 minutes or until greens are wilted and tender. Stir bacon into greens just before serving. **Yield: 12 to 15 servings.**

Fix It Faster: Forego the thick-cut bacon and use fully cooked bacon slices, which reheats in a hot skillet or microwave in 1 minute or less. You'll want to use 8 slices of fully cooked bacon since it's thinner. Use 3 Tbsp. vegetable oil in place of bacon drippings to sauté onion and celery. And you can use prechopped onion and celery.

editor's favorite
Bread Pudding with Rum Sauce

Day-old bread is best for soaking up the liquid in this comforting dessert. The easy rum sauce makes each serving luscious.

Prep: 15 min.   Cook: 50 min.

4   large eggs
1½   cups sugar
3   (12-oz.) cans evaporated milk
½   cup butter, melted
1   Tbsp. vanilla extract
2   tsp. ground cinnamon
6   cups torn, packed French bread
1   large Granny Smith apple, peeled and chopped
1   cup chopped walnuts, toasted
½   cup golden raisins
Rum Sauce

Whisk eggs in a large bowl. Whisk in sugar and next 4 ingredients. Fold in bread and next 3 ingredients, stirring until bread is moistened. Pour into a 13" x 9" baking dish coated with cooking spray. Bake, uncovered, at 350° for 50 minutes or until set. Serve warm with Rum Sauce. **Yield: 12 servings.**

Rum Sauce:

Prep: 2 min.   Cook: 3 min.

2   (14-oz.) cans sweetened condensed milk
2   Tbsp. dark rum
1   Tbsp. vanilla extract

Pour condensed milk into a small saucepan; heat over medium heat until hot, stirring often. Remove from heat, and stir in rum and vanilla. Serve warm. **Yield: 2½ cups.**

Pumpkin Pie Ice Cream Fantasy

Two holiday dessert classics are swirled with caramel and pecans—what's not to love?

Prep: 10 min.   Other: 1 hr., 8 min.

1	baked pumpkin pie*
½	gal. premium vanilla ice cream (we tested with Bluebell)

Caramel topping (we tested with Smucker's)
Toasted pecan halves

Place pie in freezer for 1 hour; remove pie from freezer, and chop ¾ of pie into 1" chunks. Allow ice cream to stand about 8 to 10 minutes to slightly soften. "Chunk up" ice cream into a large bowl. Gently fold in pie chunks until blended.

To serve, scoop each serving into wine glasses or dessert bowls. Drizzle with caramel topping, and top with pecans. **Yield: 12 servings.**

*We tested with a Mrs. Smith's frozen pumpkin pie, baked according to package directions. We let it cool completely on a wire rack, and then froze it briefly for easy chopping. You can use any type of pumpkin pie here—a deli baked pie or, better yet, a homemade pumpkin pie. (In fact, this idea would also work with a baked pecan pie. Just omit the toasted pecan halves.)

FRESH *Centerpieces*

Show off your creative side with fun and easy-to-do arrangements. Use seasonal fruits, florals, and greenery for eye-catching decorations that are guaranteed to be the center of attention at your holiday table.

Easy as 1-2-3

For a fast and fabulous tabletop decoration, place small potted plants, such as these coral bead plants, in clear glass containers. There's no need to repot the plants; the plastic pots they come in will work just fine. Wrap large leaves around the plants to conceal the pots. Leaves with intricate markings such as these croton leaves add a pretty detail.

A Little Lagniappe

Style a basketful of good wishes with this harvest decoration (facing page). Fashion small nosegays of flowers, berries, and leaves. Tie a personalized tag on each, tucking the tag into the bouquet to keep it from getting wet. Hide a vase of water in a basket; arrange bouquets inside. Pull bouquets from the basket to give to departing guests. (See page 44 for a different take on this idea.)

Simply Scent-sational

Decorate fresh oranges with whole cloves for a beautifully simple display that will fill the air with a delicious aroma (facing page). Push the cloves into the oranges to create patterns or a random design. Tie ribbons around the fruits and stack them in a bowl. Look for whole cloves in your grocery's spice section. The oranges will last for about a week.

Fast and Fabulous

Who knew elegance could be so easy? For this design, a bubble-shaped vase works best, and tulips, with their gracefully curving stems, are perfectly suited to the vase's rounded shape (below). Grapevines hold the stems in place and make this arrangement a cinch, even for beginners!

Here's How

Cut a few lengths of vine from a grapevine wreath or garland and bend the vines around the inside of the vase, crossing them over each other to form a gridlike dome (photo 1). Add water about a third of the way up the vase. Trim flower stems, leaving some stems longer to add height. Arrange flowers in the vase (photo 2).

Clear Winner

Here's a smart way to get the classic fruit-and-candle-in-a-vase look while using a lot less fruit. Gather straight-sided glass vases in varying sizes. Place a small vase inside a slightly larger one. (There needs to be an inch or so of space between the two vases.) Drop citrus slices or cranberries into the space between the vases, then add water to the top of the fruit. Fill the interior vase with water, and float a candle on top. Group several vases together on a tray or platter for a twinkling display. Look for inexpensive vases at crafts and discount stores.

Going Green

Fill a large container with moss and berries for a long-lasting showpiece. To begin, place moist florist foam in the container (if necessary, fill the bottom with crumpled newspaper, plastic bags, or bubble wrap). Lay moss on top of the foam, securing with florist pins if necessary. Stick long berry stems through the moss and into the foam. Scatter moss balls around the base of the container. For longest-lasting results, place out of direct sunlight.

Enjoy this arrangement long after the holidays are past; just remove the berry stems and leave the moss in place.

Here's How

To make moss balls, wrap bun, sheet, or reindeer moss around florist foam or plastic craft foam balls. Secure with U-shaped florist pins. Look for moss at crafts stores.

Here's How

To make the party favor bouquets, you'll need long-stemmed flowers and berries; large, flat leaves, such as cast-iron plant; and raffia or twine. To begin, gather several stems of flowers and berries together and surround them with the large leaves. Fold down the top of each leaf to the outside of the bouquet (photo 1).

Tie the arrangement together with raffia (photo 2). Repeat to make a bouquet for each guest.

Fill a vase or bowl with water. Use a knife to cut each bouquet to a suitable height for the container. If you like, you can tie a gift tag to each bouquet, but be sure to tuck it up inside the leaves so that it won't get wet. Arrange the bouquets in the water-filled container (photo 3).

Floral Favors
Line up square glass vases on a tabletop or use a large glass bowl for a centerpiece that holds petite party favors. The flowers add a festive note to the table, and guests will be delighted as you present them their own small bouquet to take home.

HOLIDAY *Tables*

Set a festive dining table to instantly make the whole house feel ready for the season.
Be inspired by the ideas on these pages—they blend traditional and trendy elements
so they're versatile enough to suit your style, whatever it may be.

Sparkly Setting

Create a showstopping centerpiece by arranging elements that share a similar color, as in this tablescape where silver sets the tone. Inject a lively air with mirrored and glittery trees and stars that reflect the twinkle and glow of the candles. Soften the look with a whisper of color as seen in the silvery green pillar candles and soft mint tablecloth. As with any grouping, add interest by using pieces that are different shapes and heights. Tuck in wisps of fresh greenery along the table so all the pieces are viewed as one big, beautiful decoration. When you have a dazzling centerpiece, use neutral-colored dinnerware to keep it from competing with the arrangement.

Traditional Tones

Plan your centerpiece using Christmassy red and green, and the cheery mood is almost instantaneous. Use pine green pillar candles to complement bright red pottery vases. Dress up the combo with a sprightly collar of greenery, flowers, and fruits, and your table's all set!

1

2

3

Here's How

This is one of the simplest and most versatile decorations you'll create for the holidays. It adapts easily to any size container, any style of materials, and it will last for several days. It can be either dressy or casual, depending on your choice of materials. For each arrangement, you'll need a container, a pillar candle, florist foam and picks, and your choice of flowers, berries, fruits, and greenery (photo 1).

Fill the container with moist florist foam. Stick stems of greenery, berries, and blooms into the foam around the outside of the container opening. Use florist picks to secure the fruit (photo 2). Set the candle in the center of the container on top of the foam. Continue adding greenery, flowers, and berries to fill in around the candle (photo 3).

Add a little water to the florist foam as needed to keep it moist. This will prolong the life of the arrangement. Be sure to protect surfaces underneath the arrangement from dampness.

Dressed-up Casual

Give rustic twig balls a makeover. Stuff them with tinsel garland and tie them with ribbons. Arrange several in a mix of sizes on a tabletop along with sturdy candleholders. Use one or more of the candleholders to elevate the twig balls for variety.

Snowy and Bright

Oh what fun it is to set a playful table that looks so
brisk and wintry! Set the scene with glass tableware.
Add a touch of frost with silvery goblets, and let
gold-tone ornaments suggest a hint of warm sunshine.

1

2

3

Here's How

To evoke the magic of a winter wonderland right on your tabletop, use lots of clear tableware and accent pieces, such as glass ornaments, vases, and cake or pastry stands. Trail an ornament garland down the center of the table to add sparkle (photo 1).

For the centerpiece, fill a tall vase with artificial snow, and use it to anchor twigs you've spray-painted white. Dust the tabletop with a sprinkling of snow. Use a pastry stand to showcase an iridescent ornament on "freshly fallen" snow. Slender pastry stands are small enough to see around easily, and their height makes the table decoration more interesting (photo 2).

For place cards, place an ornament and name tag underneath an inverted wineglass, and invite guests to take their ornament home as a special treat. Encircle the wineglass with an icy-looking bead garland (photo 3).

Season's Greetings

Let your tabletop send a message of cheer. Affix holiday quotes, poems, and phrases to clear vases and containers. Use your computer and print on vellum paper to create personalized messages, or purchase ready-made booklets of vellum sayings at crafts stores.

Here's How

Trim around the phrases, as desired, and use spray adhesive to affix the vellum cutouts to the glass. For easy placement, use a repositionable spray adhesive. Once adhered, the vellum is not easy to remove.

Painting 101

Set free your inner artist! Painting glass tableware for the holidays can be a fun family activity. Decide on a design that uses simple shapes such as dots, stripes, trees, or stars. Then decide what you want to paint—clear glass vases, domes, candleholders, and plates are good options and often can be purchased inexpensively at crafts and discount stores. Be sure to choose a nontoxic paint. If you want your design to be permanent, use paint specifically designed for painting glass; otherwise, you can scratch the painted design off with your fingernail after the holidays. Hand washing is recommended.

Table Favors

Give family and friends a special treat when they come to your holiday table. For inspiration, visit crafts and discount stores where you'll find fun items that can be combined in all sorts of imaginative ways, such as hanging a place card from a bud vase. The ideas on these two pages will get you started.

Here's How

Make a big impression with small details, such as a clutch of ornaments fastened to a chair or a cinnamon stick and greenery sprig tied to a napkin. Extend a warm welcome with a handwritten holiday greeting in an envelope personalized with rub-on transfers, or fill bags with confetti to start the celebration in style.

WHEN CRISP, COOL DAYS TURN YOUR THOUGHTS TO CHRISTMAS, LET
THE IDEAS ON THESE PAGES INSPIRE TERRIFIC HOLIDAY TRIMMINGS.

Decorating

DOOR *Decorations*

Whether adorned with a simple wreath or an over-the-top design with hundreds of lights, your front door sets the tone for your home's holiday look. These pages offer fresh, uncomplicated ideas that are quick, easy, and fun.

Garden-fresh Greetings

"Plant" a wreath that will bring a hint of spring to your front door. Line a wire wreath form (photo 1) with sheet moss, leaving open areas in the moss. Tuck small plants such as pansies, lettuce, and herbs through the openings to decorate the front of the wreath (photo 2). Fill in behind the plants with potting soil, and cover the soil with sheet moss. Attach the back of the wreath form to the wreath. Mist or water the wreath as needed to keep the plants fresh.

Pinecone Pizzazz

Extra-large sugar pinecones are striking on their own, but when you pair them with a pretty hanging vase filled with bright berries and greenery, you've got a stunning door decoration (facing page). Use wire to hold the separate elements together. In lieu of a hanging vase, you can use elongated finial-style ornaments and wire snips of greenery and berries at the tops of the ornaments. Wire a bow to the top of the arrangement and trail lengths of ribbons so they fall gracefully alongside the pinecones.

Simple Style

You can put this easy ornament decoration together in minutes (top right). After you make one for the front door, make smaller versions to hang from the mantel. Use a variety of large and small ornaments. Glue strips of ribbons around the ornaments, as desired. Loop rickrack or ribbon through the ornament hangers, and use a large safety pin to secure the ends. Pin or wire a bow at the top. Use the safety pin as a hanger.

Wintry Welcome

You can have a white Christmas even in the South (bottom right). Lay an evergreen wreath on the porch, and set tall glass vases in varying heights in the center. Fill the vases about half full with artificial snow. Place long twigs in each vase, anchoring the twigs in the snow. Sprinkle snow on the wreath, and tie ribbons around the vases. Look for long twigs at home decorating and crafts stores, or gather them from your backyard.

Have plenty of natural materials, pretty ribbons, and sparkly ornaments on hand to make holiday decorating a breeze.

Chic and Classic

Greet family and friends with a distinctive Southern accent. Magnolia leaves—a time-honored regional favorite for holiday decorating—come together in a simple swag that's the essence of elegance. If you're lucky enough to have a magnolia tree or a friendly neighbor who does, clip enough branches to form a swag that's the right size for your door.

Here's How

Start with a longer branch that can act as the backing for your arrangement. It will give a good base for attaching the other branches. Use paddle wire to bind the branches together, wrapping the wire around each branch, then wrapping the entire bundle. Turn some of the branches over so the warm bronze underside shows. Wire in stems of berries and curly willow, as desired. Tie a bow at the top of the swag.

WINSOME *Wreaths*

Hang a wreath for an instant way to make a room look holiday ready.
On these pages we show seven different looks for indoors and out.
You're sure to find a style that's right for you.

Nostalgic Noel

The simple joy of gumdrops makes this wreath a favorite with all ages. Jumbo red, white, and green candies and a jaunty polka-dot bow distinguish its charm.

To make the wreath, you'll need a plastic craft foam wreath form, masking tape, wire, wooden picks, gumdrops, and ribbon—the quantities needed will depend on the size of the wreath form. Begin by wrapping masking tape around what will be the top of the wreath. The tape reinforces the wreath for hanging. Wrap wire around the wreath over the tape, bending the wire into a hanging loop at the back of the wreath. Break wooden picks in half, inserting the broken ends into the gumdrops. Cover the top and sides of the wreath with gumdrops. Tie a bow at the top of the wreath, hiding the wire.

A Plate Full of Cheer

Give a favorite holiday plate the star treatment by framing it with a fluffy evergreen wreath (facing page). Attach a wire plate hanger to the plate, and place the plate in the center of the wreath. Wire the wreath to the plate hanger. Wire or tie a bow at the top.

Pretty Ribbons

A satiny ribbon wreath feels right at home in the bedroom (above). Select ribbons in colors that coordinate with your room's colors, and you may be tempted to leave the wreath hanging year-round. Using pins to attach the ribbons, rather than tying them around the wreath, means you use less ribbon and offers the perfect opportunity to use all those snippets you couldn't bear to throw away.

Here's How

To make the wreath, you'll need a plastic craft foam wreath form, ribbons, U-shaped florist pins, and straight pins (for narrow ribbon). Start by tying a ribbon hanger at the top of the wreath (photo 1). Fold lengths of ribbon into big loops and pin them to the wreath form, covering the top and sides (photo 2).

Bunches of Berries

Create a dramatic decoration—times four! Use gardening clippers to make a cut in the side of a vine wreath. Hook another vine wreath through the cut; repeat two more times. Use wire to make a hanging loop on the back of each wreath. Tuck berries and greenery into the wreaths. Finish with a bow at the top of each wreath.

Back to Nature

Trim a plain grapevine wreath for the holidays with materials in keeping with its casual rustic look (facing page). Randomly tuck reindeer moss between the vines. Wind a velvety ribbon around the wreath, and dangle leaf ornaments from the top of the wreath to fill the center. Look for moss at crafts and hobby stores.

Personal Statement

Make your wreath uniquely yours by using it to frame your initial (top right). Decide whether a rectangular or circular wreath is best suited for the letter you want to use. A wreath that's made on a florist foam form that has a sturdy plastic base works best because it gives you a solid surface for attaching the letter. Use adhesive putty on the back side of the letter to attach the letter to the wreath. As an alternative, hang the letter on the door; then hang the wreath so it surrounds the letter. Look for materials, including letters, at crafts and hobby stores.

Send a Message

Attach a small chalkboard to your wreath to convey a merry greeting to passersby (bottom right). Use the board to write best wishes for the holidays, an invitation to a neighborhood open house, or even reminders to the family.

Mist evergreen wreaths every couple of days to keep them fresh and green throughout the season.

GREAT *Garlands*

Be it fragrant festoons of evergreens or swags of popcorn and cranberries, garlands are mainstays of Christmas decorating. Take a look at these enchanting interpretations to spark your imagination for your own creative designs.

Trendy Blend

Pair a Christmas classic—a grand holly garland—with fashionable accents for an updated mantel style. Let citrus fruits spark the color scheme for flowers and candles in shades of red, orange, and green. Stack a pyramid of oranges in a large container to enhance the hearth. Use florist picks to hold the oranges in place.

Easy Does It

Don't you love it when the most simple idea results in a fabulous finish? Create a dazzling stairway decoration simply by adding ornaments to an evergreen garland (left). Embellishing the garland with anything else would take away from the simple charm. Just place the garland, and hang the ornaments. You'll be finished in minutes! If necessary, use more than one ornament hanger so the entire ornament hangs beneath the garland.

All in a Row

If you don't have a mantel or you just want to do something different this year, hang your stockings in a window (below). Trim the display with beaded garlands for a double-duty decoration that looks good both indoors and out. Tie fluffy bows at the ends of the garland for a pretty finish.

Cute Countdown

String this whimsical advent garland for a fun way to tick off the days 'til Christmas. Recruit the kids to help cut out designs from decorative papers and recycled holiday cards to glue on tiny gift bags. Fill the bags with small surprises that lead right up to the big day. Look for materials at crafts and discount stores.

Here's How
To make the advent garland, decorate small gift bags with paper cutouts and stickers. Number the bags from 1 to 25, using numbers cut from paper or rub-on transfers. Fill the bags with small treats, and then use ribbons and clothespins to attach the bags to twine.

To All a Goodnight

Cozy-up the bedroom with a lighthearted garland made by stringing together ornaments and small stockings on a ribbon. Tie the garland to the footboard of the bed (facing page). Enhance the garland decoration with a coordinating wreath (below). The ornaments and wreath shown here are made from recycled fabric scraps and are so cuddly you'd be tempted to snuggle up with them for a long winter's nap, making them perfect accessories for the bedroom.

A MEDLEY OF *Mantels*

A fireplace naturally draws your attention, so it's a logical place to concentrate your very best seasonal decorating efforts. Open the cabinets and closets and use your favorite things for an effortless way to make the most of this choice spot.

Enchanted Forest

For an impressive display, set a theme using decorative items that share similar characteristics. For a woodsy mood, use bronze-colored items such as the trees and candleholders (facing page). Add a dramatic piece, such as the reindeer, to make the grouping more interesting. Give your arrangement the requisite seasonal sparkle with glittery pillar candles, glistening garlands, and metallic ribbons. Then bring all the elements together on a foundation of evergreen garland or clippings. Wire lengths of wired ribbon along the garland to fill in the empty spaces and to add pops of color.

Natural Glow

Take a nature walk and gather the materials for this simply elegant mantel. Place creamy pillar candles in tall glass vases and encircle them with magnolia leaves, alternating the leaves in a front-and-back fashion to show off the beautiful contrasting colors. Place pinecones and votive candles between the vases to light up the scene. Be sure to place magnolia leaves and pinecones well away from candle flames and never leave burning candles unattended.

Fancy Votive Holders

Dress up clear votive holders for their seasonal debut. Cut a length of wide ribbon long enough to wrap around the votive holder with a bit of overlap. Use a hot-glue gun to glue the ends together. The ribbon wrappings help the clear votive holders blend with the arrangement and give the candles a warm, golden glow.

Pretty Presentation

Here's an easy and inexpensive way to get the added height you need for a nicely balanced mantel decoration (above). Tie ribbon around a stack of wrapped gift boxes, and place the stack atop a cake stand, urn, or any container that has a pedestal base. Place a stack at each end of the mantel. Fill in with small wrapped packages and vases filled with candies and candles.

By the Sea

If you spend the season at the shore or just love the nautical look, gather your beach treasures and use them for an out-of-the-ordinary holiday array (top right). To make a seashell tree, adhere heavy linen fabric to a sturdy backing, such as cardboard, and then glue shells in a tree shape on the linen, finishing with a starfish topper. Frame, as desired.

Bright and Easy

For a cheery burst of color on the mantel, fill containers with moist florist foam and stick in stems of red holly berries (bottom right). Hang miniature ornaments from the branches, and nestle larger ornaments amid greenery clippings placed on the mantel.

Buckets of Goodies

Opt for pretty pails this year instead of the usual stockings. For easy identification, tie a small wooden letter to each one. Wire cedar clippings into circles and place at the top of the buckets (below). For the days leading up to Christmas, fill the buckets with greenery, candy canes, ornaments, and small wrapped packages. On Christmas Eve, take away the decorations, leaving the buckets ready for Santa's visit. Look for metal pails and wooden letters at crafts and hobby stores.

Classic Colors

The traditional holiday color scheme of bright red and green is made modern with vases filled with vivid red tulips. For informal flair, use pottery vases for the flowers. Embellish the evergreen garland with sprigs of variegated holly to continue the red-and-green theme.

INSPIRED BY *Nature*

Let the great outdoors lend a hand with your holiday decorating. Woodsy hues become warm and golden against winter evergreens, and nothing evokes Christmas like the fragrance of freshly cut greenery. Use copper accessories for shimmery highlights.

Create a Scene

Stir up a little drama by planning decorations with the mood of your setting in mind. For a natural stone fireplace with a rough-hewn mantel, consider rustic accessories such as twiggy birdhouses and birch bark candles. Continue the theme by wiring tiny birdhouses and birds nests to wreaths suspended from the mantel. Fill copper containers with potted evergreens from the nursery (after the holidays you can plant them in your yard). Use one container as a bold accent on the mantel and place another on the hearth to incorporate the entire fireplace into the grouping. Add interest to the mantel arrangement by varying the heights of the pieces. Use a small stool or a stack of books where you need elevation.

Pole Position

Suspend wreaths below the mantel to fill in the gap between the mantel and the fire screen. For a unique approach, use a limb or birch pole to hold the wreaths. For best results, use lightweight wreaths, such as vine wreaths. Shown here are vine wreaths with seeded eucalyptus tucked between the vines. Add interest to the centers of the wreaths by attaching small items such as the birdhouses and bird's nest. Or wire an ornament or bells to the wreath to suit the same purpose. Finish with ribbons in colors that complement the overall arrangement. Here, the soft green and brown ribbons subtly enrich the setting.

Here's How

To hang the birch pole from the mantel, loop a length of ribbon around the pole, and use a heavy-duty upholstery tack to attach the ribbon to the mantel (photo 1). Wire the wreaths to the pole, and tie ribbon around the pole to hide the wire (photo 2).

Add Interest

Since the mantel is usually the most attention-getting feature in a room, make it an intriguing gazing point by filling it with a variety of shapes and textures (above). Fill twig balls with reindeer moss for an easy way to add shape, texture, and color. Use a pencil to poke the moss into the center of the ball. Reindeer moss is a bright chartreuse and is sold by the bag at crafts and discount stores.

Fill in the Details

Tuck sheet moss around the items on the mantel to give it a finished look (right). You can find moss in bags at crafts and discount stores. The moss is dry and shouldn't cause any harm, but you may want to cover the mantel with a sheet of plastic, such as a large trash bag, to play it safe. Just tuck the edges underneath the moss to hide the plastic. After Christmas, the plastic will make a neater job of removing the moss.

Using natural materials, such as potted evergreens, moss, and wood, instantly sets a casual theme and makes holiday decorating easy and inexpensive.

Here's How

For a coordinated scheme, repeat materials, such as the bird's nests and eggs, throughout the house and even in the table settings.

LETTER *Perfect*

Personalizing items, whether with monograms or meaningful phrases, makes them all the more special—especially during the holidays. Here, we show several ideas that will help you express yourself in a most attractive way.

Play Tag

Use your table setting to convey a seasonal greeting by spelling out a phrase using rubber stamps and small paper luggage tags. Stamp one letter per tag, thread a thin ribbon through the hole in the tag, and tie it to a rolled napkin. Line up the napkins on a large platter or on the tabletop to spell out a sentiment such as Happy New Year, Merry Christmas, peace, or noel.

Rub-on alphabet transfers work well as an alternative to rubber stamps, and the alphabet sheets often include punctuation and decorative dingbats, so you can add embellishments to your tags. Look for rubber stamps, rub-on transfers, and blank luggage tags at crafts, discount, and scrapbooking stores.

Christmastime Frame

Deck the walls with framed letters spelling out a festive phrase. Use purchased alphabet cards, or create your own cards by using rub-on transfers or by printing letters from your computer onto sturdy paper. If you prefer, frame illustrations from last year's Christmas cards instead of letters. For a seasonal arrangement, lean the frames against the wall or prop them on plate stands to avoid unnecessary nail holes. Look for inexpensive frames at crafts and discount stores, or use frames you already have. You can easily remove the letters after the holidays.

Here's How

To frame letters, glue each card to a sheet of decorative paper, such as scrapbooking paper (photo 1). Place each letter in a separate frame. Use a variety of different-sized frames with complementary designs for an interesting presentation (photo 2).

Harvest-to-Christmas Door Decor

Let your harvest decoration transcend the season with just a few simple changes. Set a pumpkin atop an urn or other large container. For autumn, anchor branches of colored leaves, berries, and seed pods underneath the pumpkin, forming a collar (above). Place gourds and small pumpkins around the base of the container. For Christmas, replace the harvest-colored foliage with rich evergreens, such as magnolia leaves and cedar branches (facing page). Tuck in berries to add pops of color and texture. Surround the container's base with clippings.

Here's How

For autumn, display your pumpkin unpainted, or spray paint it metallic gold (above). At Christmastime, paint the pumpkin a creamy white for a dramatic contrast with the evergreen trimmings. Hand-paint your initial for a personal touch.

INDULGE IN THIS SLEIGHFUL OF OFFERINGS FOR YOUR HOLIDAY
TABLE, FEATURING CLASSIC BAKING RECIPES, HALF-HOUR ENTRÉES,
EASY SIDE DISHES, AND CHOCOLATE AND VANILLA SURPRISES. TURN
THE PAGE TO BEGIN WITH SOME TRULY SIMPLE CHRISTMAS RECIPES.

Recipes

SIMPLE *Christmas*

Keep things simple this holiday season. Start with these innovative and practically effortless recipes to stir you toward your goal.

editor's favorite • quick & easy

Honey-Roasted Grape Tomato Crostini

Prep: 2 min. Cook: 20 min.

1   pt. grape tomatoes
1   Tbsp. honey
1½ tsp. olive oil
¼   tsp. kosher salt
1   (4-oz.) log goat cheese
1   (6- to 8-oz.) container crostini*
Garnish: fresh rosemary

Toss together first 3 ingredients on a lightly greased rimmed baking sheet. Bake at 450° for 20 minutes or until tomato skins burst and begin to wrinkle (do not stir). Transfer roasted tomatoes to a bowl, scraping accumulated juices into bowl. Stir salt into tomato mixture.

Microwave goat cheese at HIGH 8 to 10 seconds to soften. Smear goat cheese evenly over crostini; top with roasted tomatoes. Serve on a platter; garnish, if desired. **Yield: 31 crostini.**

*We found numerous sizes of crostini packages available at large grocery chains. Look for a 6- to 8-oz. container so that you'll have plenty for this recipe. Enjoy any leftovers as croutons over salad greens.

quick & easy

Parmesan-Peppercorn Snowflakes

These delicate, cheesy gems are perfect for an appetizer buffet served alongside mixed nuts and olives.

Prep: 7 min. Cook: 6 min.

2   cups freshly shredded Parmigiano-Reggiano cheese
½   tsp. crushed tricolor peppercorn blend

Drop cheese by slightly heaping tablespoonfuls onto parchment paper-lined baking sheets, and spread into 3½" rounds. Sprinkle each portion of cheese lightly with crushed peppercorns. Bake at 425° for 5 to 6 minutes or until bubbly and browned. Cool for 2 to 3 minutes on baking sheets. Remove with a metal spatula to wire racks to cool completely (cheese crisps up as it cools). **Yield: 20 snowflakes.**

gift idea

Rosemary-Lemon Olives

The infused oil resulting from this recipe is great for dipping crusty baguette slices. For gift giving, replace the baked rosemary and lemon peel with fresh sprigs of rosemary and fresh lemon peel.

Prep: 4 min. Cook: 40 min.

6   (5") strips lemon peel
2   (8") fresh rosemary sprigs
⅛   tsp. crushed red pepper flakes
1   cup kalamata olives
1   cup Sicilian olives
1   cup extra virgin olive oil
Garnish: fresh rosemary

Place lemon peel, rosemary, and red pepper flakes in an 11" x 7" baking dish. Add olives, and drizzle with olive oil. Bake, uncovered, at 300° for 40 minutes. Cool to room temperature. Garnish, if desired, and serve immediately, or store in refrigerator up to 5 days. Bring refrigerated olives to room temperature before serving. **Yield: 2 cups.**

Creole Fried Bow-Ties

This crispy snack is simply pasta that's cooked and then tossed in a spicy cornmeal coating and quickly fried. Serve these nibbles hot or at room temperature.

Prep: 7 min. Cook: 4 min. per batch

8   oz. bow-tie pasta
⅓   cup yellow cornmeal
3   Tbsp. spicy Creole seasoning (we tested with
     Tony Chachere's More Spice Creole Seasoning)
Vegetable oil

Cook pasta according to package directions; drain well, and blot pasta dry with paper towels.

Combine cornmeal and Creole seasoning in a large bowl. Toss pasta, a handful at a time, in cornmeal mixture to coat; shake off excess.

Pour oil to a depth of 2" in a Dutch oven; heat over medium-high heat to 375°. Fry pasta, in batches, 3 to 4 minutes or until golden brown. Drain on paper towels. Store pasta snacks up to a week in an airtight container. **Yield: 6 cups.**

Creole Fried Bow-Ties

Balsamic-Splashed Bacon and Arugula Canapés

Ricotta salata is a dry salted ricotta cheese that can be found in specialty grocery stores.

Prep: 9 min. Cook: 5 min.

6   fully cooked bacon slices
2   tsp. honey
⅛   tsp. ground red pepper
12   (½"-thick) French baguette slices, lightly toasted
24   arugula leaves
12   thinly shaved pieces ricotta salata or Parmesan cheese
2   Tbsp. balsamic glaze (we tested with Gia Russa)*

Place bacon on a baking sheet lined with aluminum foil. Combine honey and pepper; brush onto bacon. Bake at 375° for 5 minutes or until hot. Cut bacon in half crosswise.

Place baguette slices on a serving platter; top with arugula leaves. Arrange bacon and cheese on arugula. Drizzle each canapé with ½ tsp. balsamic glaze. Serve immediately. **Yield: 1 dozen.**

*Make your own balsamic glaze by reducing balsamic vinegar. Cook ½ cup balsamic vinegar in a small saucepan over medium heat 9 minutes or until syrupy and reduced to 3 Tbsp. Cool completely.

Tuna Niçoise Canapés

Prep: 15 min.

2   (5.5-oz.) cans solid light tuna in olive oil, well
     drained and flaked (we tested with Starkist)
¼   cup finely minced red onion
3   Tbsp. chopped kalamata or niçoise olives
2   Tbsp. capers, drained
2   tsp. extra virgin olive oil
2   tsp. Dijon mustard
2   tsp. balsamic vinegar
¼   to ½ tsp. freshly ground pepper
⅛   tsp. kosher salt
Endive leaves or cucumber slices
Garnishes: sliced kalamata olives, fresh flat-leaf parsley

Combine first 9 ingredients in a medium bowl. To serve, spoon tuna mixture onto endive leaves or cucumber slices. Garnish, if desired. **Yield: about 3 dozen.**

Pecan, Olive, and Parmesan Rugelach

Rugelach, traditionally a Jewish pastry, is often filled with nuts and raisins or preserves. This easy savory takeoff is best served warm from the oven.

Prep: 12 min.   Cook: 15 min.

⅓ cup finely chopped pecans, toasted
⅓ cup finely chopped imported green olives
    (we tested with Picholine)
¼ cup freshly grated Parmesan cheese
2 tsp. minced fresh thyme
1 (8-oz.) can refrigerated crescent rolls
Paprika

Combine first 4 ingredients in a medium bowl.
Unroll crescent rolls onto a lightly floured cutting board. Sprinkle pecan mixture evenly over dough, pressing firmly into dough. Using a sharp knife, cut dough along perforations. Cut each triangle lengthwise into 2 equal triangles.
Roll up each triangle, starting at wide end. Place rugelach, point sides down, on an ungreased baking sheet, curving them into a crescent shape. Sprinkle with paprika. Bake at 375° for 15 minutes or until browned. Serve hot. **Yield: 16 pastries.**

1. Sprinkle pecan mixture over dough.   2. Press ingredients firmly into dough.

3. Cut each triangle lengthwise into 2 equal triangles. Roll up each triangle, starting at wide end.

Jalapeño-Cheese Sausage Cups

Serve these spicy sausage cups as pick-up food for a ball game get-together.

Prep: 9 min.   Cook: 14 min.

1 lb. hot ground pork sausage
½ cup Ranch dressing
2 (2.1-oz.) packages frozen mini-phyllo pastry shells, thawed
½ cup pickled jalapeño slices, drained
½ cup shredded sharp Cheddar cheese

Brown sausage in a large skillet over medium-high heat, stirring to crumble; drain. Return sausage to skillet; stir in Ranch dressing. Spoon sausage mixture evenly into phyllo shells. Place shells on a baking sheet. Top sausage cups evenly with pepper slices; sprinkle with cheese. Bake at 350° for 8 to 10 minutes or until pastry shells are browned. **Yield: 30 appetizers.**

Ranch Popcorn

This flavored popcorn is addictive.

Prep: 1 min.   Cook: 2 min.

1 (3-oz.) bag butter-flavored 94% fat-free popped microwave popcorn (we tested with Pop Secret)
Butter-flavored cooking spray
1½ Tbsp. Ranch dressing mix

Pour popped corn into a large bowl; coat heavily with cooking spray. Sprinkle Ranch dressing mix over popcorn; toss well. **Yield: 9½ cups.**

Bloody Mary Shrimp Cocktail

Pile these spicy marinated shrimp in martini glasses for a fun way to present a classic appetizer.

Prep: 12 min.   Cook: 5 min.   Other: 8 hr.

1   lb. unpeeled, large raw shrimp (about 30)
1   cup hot and spicy Bloody Mary cocktail mix
¼   cup chopped Spanish olives
1   to 2 Tbsp. capers, drained
Garnishes: pimiento-stuffed Spanish olives, celery leaves

   Bring 3 qt. water to a boil; add shrimp, and cook 3 to 5 minutes or just until shrimp turn pink. Drain and rinse with cold water. Peel shrimp.
   Combine shrimp and cocktail mix in a large zip-top plastic freezer bag. Seal bag, and chill 8 hours.
   Remove shrimp from marinade; discard marinade. For a fun presentation, divide shrimp among martini glasses. Sprinkle each serving with chopped olives and capers. Garnish, if desired. **Yield: 4 to 6 appetizer servings.**

editor's favorite • quick & easy
Pesto Chicken Quesadillas

These skillet quesadillas are quick and delicious. Try a flavored rotisserie chicken or add some toasted pine nuts to kick up the flavor. Marinara or sour cream makes a nice dollop on the plate.

Prep: 13 min.   Cook: 4 min. per batch

1   (3.5-oz.) jar pesto (we tested with Alessi)
4   (8") flour tortillas
1½   cups shredded rotisserie chicken
1   (8-oz.) package shredded Italian cheese blend
Softened butter or yogurt-based spread (we tested with
       Brummel & Brown)

   Spread about 1½ Tbsp. pesto on each tortilla. Sprinkle a slightly heaping ⅓ cup chicken onto half of each tortilla; sprinkle cheese over chicken on each tortilla.
   Fold each tortilla in half. Butter both sides of each folded tortilla.
   Heat a large nonstick skillet over medium-high heat. Cook quesadillas, in 2 batches, 2 minutes on each side or until browned and crusty. Remove to a cutting board, and cut each quesadilla into 3 wedges. **Yield: 2 to 4 servings.**

Chicken Yakitori

Yakitori is a Japanese grilled chicken skewer that makes a great party appetizer-on-a-stick and goes well with Japanese beer.

Prep: 11 min.   Cook: 8 min.   Other: 30 min.

6   green onions
½   cup teriyaki marinade and sauce (we tested
       with Kikkoman)
1½   Tbsp. grated fresh ginger
2   large garlic cloves, pressed
1   Tbsp. sugar
2   Tbsp. dark sesame oil
1   lb. boneless, skinless chicken breast, cut into 1" pieces

   Cut white and pale green parts of green onions into 1½" pieces. Thinly slice dark green onion tops. Set aside.
   Combine marinade, ginger, garlic, sugar, and sesame oil in a zip-top plastic freezer bag; add chicken and 1½" green onion pieces, turning to coat. Seal and chill for at least 30 minutes or up to 2 hours.
   Meanwhile, soak 8 (6") wooden skewers in water to cover for 30 minutes. Drain.
   Thread marinated chicken and green onion pieces onto skewers, discarding marinade. Grill over medium-high heat (350° to 400°) for 3 to 4 minutes on each side or until chicken is done.
   Transfer skewers to an appetizer platter, and sprinkle with thinly sliced green onions. **Yield: 8 appetizer servings.**

editor's favorite
Pimiento Cheese Fondue

Prep: 9 min.   Cook: 2 hr.

4   cups (16 oz.) shredded extra-sharp Cheddar cheese
1   (8-oz.) package cream cheese, softened
1   cup heavy whipping cream
1   (7-oz.) jar diced pimiento, well drained
¼   cup thinly sliced green onions
¼   tsp. ground red pepper

   Combine first 3 ingredients in a 3- or 4-qt. slow cooker. Cover and cook on LOW 1 hour. Stir to combine. Cover and cook on LOW 30 more minutes. Add pimiento, green onions, and red pepper. Stir to blend. Cover and cook on LOW 30 more minutes or until thoroughly heated. Serve fondue with raw vegetables, tortilla chips, or French bread chunks. **Yield: 4 cups.**

Blue Chip Nachos

Your favorite blue cheese is essential for decadence here.

Prep: 12 min.   Cook: 5 min.

1   (4-oz.) wedge Maytag or other blue cheese
3   Tbsp. tub-style cream cheese, softened
⅓   cup whipping cream
1   (5-oz.) bag lightly salted crinkle-cut potato chips
    (we tested with Kettle brand)
1   cup chopped walnuts, toasted
2   tsp. chopped fresh thyme
2   tsp. chopped fresh rosemary
2   to 3 Tbsp. bottled balsamic glaze (we tested with
    Gia Russa)

Combine cheeses and whipping cream in a small bowl, stirring well. Spread whole potato chips in a double layer on a parchment paper-lined baking sheet. Dollop cheese onto potato chips. Sprinkle with walnuts. Bake at 400° for 5 minutes or until heated. Remove from oven, and carefully slide chips and parchment paper onto a wooden board. Sprinkle with herbs; drizzle with desired amount of balsamic glaze. Serve immediately. **Yield: 8 to 10 servings.**

Chocolate-Caramel-Pecan Potato Chips

These chips are best served the day they're made. Use the thickest ridged potato chips you can find.

Prep: 34 min.   Cook: 12 min.

1   (13-oz.) bag thick ruffled potato chips (we tested
    with Wavy Lays)
1   (14-oz.) bag caramels (we tested with Kraft)
⅓   cup whipping cream
1   (11.5-oz.) bag milk chocolate morsels
2   Tbsp. shortening
1   cup finely chopped pecans, toasted

Spread whole potato chips in single layers on parchment paper-lined wire racks. Combine caramels and cream in a heavy saucepan over low heat, stirring constantly, until smooth; remove from heat. Drizzle caramel over chips.

Melt milk chocolate morsels and shortening in a small bowl in microwave at HIGH, 1½ to 2 minutes, stirring after 1 minute; cool slightly. Drizzle chocolate over caramel on potato chips; sprinkle with pecans. Cool until chocolate and caramel harden. **Yield: about 9 dozen.**

Blue Chip Nachos

Potato chips prove their panache in these two unique snacks—one's sweet, the other one's savory.

Chocolate-Caramel-Pecan Potato Chips

Grilled Shrimp Caesar

Smoked paprika is a delicious seasoning to have on hand. It's wonderful in marinades and as a seasoning for sauces and soups. It's made by smoke-drying red pepper pods before grinding and can range from sweet to spicy hot.

Prep: 7 min.   Cook: 6 min.

2	(8-oz.) packages complete Caesar salad mix (we tested with Fresh Express)
24	unpeeled, large raw shrimp
2	Tbsp. olive oil
2	Tbsp. fresh lemon juice
2	large garlic cloves, minced, or 2 tsp. jarred minced garlic
1	tsp. smoked paprika
½	tsp. salt
¼	tsp. freshly ground pepper

Empty lettuce and croutons from salad mix into a bowl; chill. Set salad dressing and Parmesan cheese packets aside.

Peel and, if desired, devein shrimp. Combine shrimp and next 6 ingredients in a bowl; toss to coat. Thread shrimp onto 4 (10") metal skewers. Grill over medium-high heat (350° to 400°) for 3 minutes on each side or just until shrimp turn pink. Remove shrimp from skewers, if desired.

Lightly toss salad with desired amount of reserved dressing. Divide salad among individual serving plates. Top each salad with 6 shrimp, and sprinkle with reserved cheese. **Yield: 4 servings.**

Baked Three-Cheese Ziti

Prep: 11 min.   Cook: 40 min.

12	oz. uncooked ziti pasta
3	cups marinara sauce
1	(8-oz.) package shredded mozzarella cheese
½	cup freshly grated Parmesan cheese
1	cup ricotta cheese
3	Tbsp. jarred pesto sauce
¼	tsp. dried crushed red pepper

Freshly grated Parmesan cheese

Cook pasta according to package directions; drain and transfer to a large bowl. Add 2 cups marinara sauce, half of mozzarella cheese, half of Parmesan cheese, ricotta cheese, pesto, and red pepper, stirring gently to blend.

Spoon pasta mixture into a lightly greased 13" x 9" baking dish. Spoon remaining marinara sauce over pasta; sprinkle with remaining mozzarella and Parmesan cheese.

Bake, uncovered, at 400° for 30 minutes or until cheese is melted and bubbly. Serve extra Parmesan at the table. **Yield: 6 to 8 servings.**

Chicken Fajitas

Prep: 12 min.   Cook: 9 min.

2	Tbsp. olive oil
1	red bell pepper, cut lengthwise into ½" strips
1	medium onion, sliced
½	tsp. ground cumin
½	tsp. salt
3	cups shredded cooked rotisserie chicken
3	Tbsp. minced fresh cilantro
1½	Tbsp. minced pickled jalapeño peppers
8	(8") flour tortillas

Toppings: salsa, guacamole, sour cream

Heat 2 Tbsp. olive oil in a large skillet over medium heat. Add bell pepper and next 3 ingredients. Cook 8 minutes or until pepper and onion are tender, stirring often. Add chicken, cilantro, and jalapeño peppers; cook 2 minutes or until thoroughly heated. Remove from heat, and keep warm.

Warm tortillas according to package directions.

Transfer chicken mixture to a serving platter. Serve with tortillas and desired toppings. **Yield: 4 servings.**

Chicken Pot Pie

This is easy comfort food with a puff pastry crust.

Prep: 9 min.   Cook: 46 min.

2	Tbsp. butter
1	small onion, minced
1	(8-oz.) pkg. sliced fresh mushrooms
½	tsp. salt
1	(10-oz.) package frozen mixed vegetables, thawed and drained
3	cups chopped rotisserie chicken
1	(10¾-oz.) can reduced-sodium cream of chicken soup
⅔	cup milk
1	to 2 Tbsp. dry sherry (optional)
1	Tbsp. fresh lemon juice
1	sheet frozen puff pastry, thawed

Melt butter in a large skillet over medium heat. Add onion and cook, stirring occasionally, 3 minutes or until tender. Add mushrooms and salt; sauté 8 minutes or until liquid evaporates and mushrooms are browned. Add vegetables and next 5 ingredients, stirring to blend.

Pour chicken mixture into a lightly greased 10" deep-dish pie plate, and cover with pastry; trim excess pastry. Bake at 375° for 30 to 35 minutes or until filling is bubbly and pastry is golden. **Yield: 6 servings.**

Apricot-Glazed Pork Tenderloin with Couscous

A two-ingredient glaze paints this pork with rich color and tangy-sweet flavor.

Prep: 10 min.   Cook: 18 min.   Other: 5 min.

1	(1¼-lb.) pork tenderloin
1	Tbsp. olive oil
¼	tsp. salt
¼	tsp. pepper
⅓	cup apricot preserves
2	Tbsp. honey mustard
1	(10-oz.) box couscous (we tested with Far East)
½	cup diced dried apricots
⅓	cup toasted sliced almonds

Brush pork with olive oil; season with salt and pepper. Place on an aluminum foil-lined broiler pan.

Broil 5½" from heat 8 minutes or until browned, turning once.

Combine apricot preserves and honey mustard; spread over pork. Continue to broil 10 more minutes, turning once, or until meat thermometer inserted in center of meat registers 155°. Cover pork with aluminum foil, and let stand 5 minutes.

Meanwhile, prepare couscous according to package directions. Fluff couscous; stir in apricots and almonds. Slice pork, and serve with couscous. **Yield: 4 servings.**

SIMPLE CHRISTMAS **115**

Chocolate Cream Martini

Brownie Buttons

quick & easy

Chocolate Cream Martini

This luxurious drink is both cocktail and dessert.

Prep: 4 min.

1   (1-oz.) square semisweet chocolate, melted
3   Tbsp. vanilla-flavored vodka (we tested with
     Absolut Vanilla)
3   Tbsp. Irish cream liqueur
2   Tbsp. half-and-half
⅓   cup coffee-flavored liqueur (we tested with
     Tia Maria)
⅓   cup chocolate-flavored liqueur (we tested with
     Godiva)

Dip rims of 2 martini glasses in melted chocolate on
a plate to form a thin layer. Place glasses in refrigerator
until chocolate is firm.

Combine vodka and next 4 ingredients in a martini
shaker filled with ice. Cover with lid; shake until thoroughly
chilled. Remove lid; strain into chocolate-rimmed martini
glasses. Serve immediately. **Yield: 2 servings.**

gift idea

Brownie Buttons

*Nestle miniature chocolate candies into freshly baked brownie
bites for impressive little chocolate treats.*

Prep: 15 min.   Cook: 20 min.   Other: 14 min.

1   (16.5-oz.) refrigerated roll triple chocolate chunk
     brownie batter (we tested with Pillsbury)
1   bag of assorted miniature peanut butter cup
     candies and chocolate-coated caramels
     (we tested with Rolos)

Spray miniature (1¾") muffin pans with cooking spray,
or line pans with paper liners and spray liners with cooking spray. Spoon brownie batter evenly into each cup,
filling almost full. Bake at 350° for 19 to 20 minutes.
Cool in pans 3 to 4 minutes, and then gently press a
miniature candy into each baked brownie until the top
of candy is level with top of brownie. Cool 10 minutes
in pans. Gently twist each brownie to remove from pan.
Cool on a wire rack. **Yield: 20 brownies.**

Hazelnut Mousse Crunch

Fudgy Toffee-Crunch Brownies

quick & easy

Hazelnut Mousse Crunch

For a special effect, use a decorative tip to pipe the mousse into each glass. All you need is a large star tip and piping bag.

Prep: 5 min.   Cook: 1 min.

1   (13-oz.) jar hazelnut spread (we tested with Nutella)
1   (8-oz.) container frozen whipped topping, thawed
1   (6.88-oz) package bittersweet chocolate-dipped biscotti or other favorite biscotti (we tested with Nonni's)

Microwave hazelnut spread, uncovered, on HIGH for 25 seconds (be sure to completely remove foil wrap). Fold hazelnut spread and whipped topping together in a large bowl, leaving some chocolate streaks. Spoon mousse into a zip-top plastic freezer bag (do not seal). Snip 1 corner of bag to make a hole. Pipe mousse into parfait glasses. Serve with biscotti; or crush biscotti, and lightly sprinkle over each serving to provide the crunch. **Yield: 6 servings.**

gift idea • make ahead

Fudgy Toffee-Crunch Brownies

No one will detect that these decadent brownies start with a mix.

Prep: 16 min.   Cook: 52 min.

2   (17.6-oz.) packages dark fudge brownie mix with chocolate chunks (we tested with Duncan Hines Chocolate Lover's)
2   large eggs
½   cup vegetable oil or canola oil
¼   cup water
1   Tbsp. instant espresso granules
1   (12-oz.) package miniature chocolate-covered toffee bars, coarsely crushed (we tested with Heath Miniatures)

Beat first 4 ingredients at medium speed with an electric mixer for 3 minutes or until blended; stir in coffee granules and candy bars. Spoon batter into a lightly greased 13" x 9" pan, spreading evenly (batter will be very thick).

Bake at 325° for 50 to 52 minutes or until center is set. Cool in pan on a wire rack. Cut into bars. **Yield: 2 dozen.**

CHOCOLATE & *Vanilla*

Chocolate and vanilla are classic dessert themes. Discover these ingredients anew with fresh and deliciously unexpected flavor pairings. Your palate will be happily surprised.

Vanilla Crumb Cakes

Prep: 14 min.   Cook: 30 min.

¼   cup plus 2 Tbsp. granulated sugar
¼   cup plus 2 Tbsp. firmly packed light brown sugar
1½ cups plus 2 Tbsp. all-purpose flour
¼   tsp. freshly grated nutmeg
½   cup unsalted butter, cut into pieces
½   cup buttermilk
1   tsp. vanilla bean paste or vanilla extract
½   tsp. baking powder
¼   tsp. baking soda
¼   tsp. salt
1   large egg
Vanilla Glaze

Stir together sugars in a large bowl. Add flour and nutmeg, whisking until blended. Cut butter into flour mixture with a pastry blender or fork until crumbly. Remove and reserve ½ cup crumb mixture.

Combine buttermilk, vanilla, baking powder, baking soda, and salt; whisk in egg. Pour over crumb mixture in large bowl; stir with a fork until dry ingredients are moistened.

Spoon batter evenly into a greased jumbo muffin pan, filling 4 muffin cups with batter. Fill 2 empty cups halfway with water. Sprinkle reserved crumb mixture evenly over batter, pressing lightly into batter. Bake at 350° for 28 to 30 minutes or until a wooden pick inserted in center comes out clean. Cool in pan on a wire rack 10 minutes; remove cakes from pan, and let cool completely on wire rack. Drizzle with Vanilla Glaze. **Yield: 4 crumb cakes.**

Vanilla Glaze:

⅔   cup powdered sugar
1   Tbsp. milk
½   tsp. vanilla bean paste or vanilla extract

Whisk all ingredients until smooth. **Yield: ¼ cup.**

Chocolate-Chipotle Fondue

make ahead • quick & easy

Chocolate-Chipotle Fondue

Popular in the 1960s, fondue keeps coming back. Try this updated version with a kick from spicy chipotle pepper. Enjoy leftovers over ice cream.

Prep: 5 min.   Cook: 11 min.

4   (4-oz.) sweet dark chocolate baking bars, chopped (we tested with Ghirardelli)
1½ cups whipping cream
½   cup canned dulce de leche (we tested with La Lechera)
1   tsp. ground chipotle chile powder
⅓   cup coffee liqueur (we tested with Kahlúa)
Dippers: Candied fruit (we tested with mango slices, papaya strips, and pineapple chunks); banana slices; pound cake cubes; marshmallows

Combine first 3 ingredients in a medium saucepan; cook, stirring constantly, over medium-low heat until chocolate melts and mixture is smooth. Stir in chile powder and coffee liqueur. Pour mixture into a fondue pot; place over fondue burner. Serve with candied fruit, banana slices, cake cubes, and marshmallows as dippers. **Yield: 3¼ cups.**

gift idea • make ahead

Deep Dark Fudge with Candied Ginger

A dab of wasabi paste gives this fudge an intriguing Asian influence.

Prep: 5 min.   Cook: 8 min.   Other: 2 hr.

1¼ cups sugar
1 (5-oz.) can evaporated milk
2 Tbsp. butter
⅛ tsp. salt
2 cups miniature marshmallows
2 tsp. wasabi paste (optional)
1⅔ cups 60% cacao bittersweet chocolate morsels (we tested with Ghirardelli)
1 tsp. vanilla extract
3 Tbsp. minced crystallized ginger

Line a lightly greased 8″ square pan with nonstick aluminum foil; set aside.

Combine first 4 ingredients in a medium-size heavy saucepan. Cook over medium heat, stirring constantly, until mixture comes to a boil; boil 4 minutes, stirring constantly. Remove from heat. Add marshmallows, wasabi paste, if desired, plus chocolate morsels, and vanilla. Beat by hand with a wooden spoon until melted and smooth. Spread fudge into prepared pan. Sprinkle top with crystallized ginger, and press lightly into fudge. Refrigerate 2 hours or until firm. Cut into squares. **Yield: 1½ lb.**

make ahead

Vanilla-Banana-Caramel Flans

Toasted walnut halves are the perfect finish for these smooth, dense custards.

Prep: 10 min.   Cook: 46 min.   Other: 8 hr.

1½ cups sugar, divided
2 small very ripe bananas
1 Tbsp. vanilla bean paste
1½ cups half-and-half
5 large eggs
6 walnut halves, toasted

Place 1 cup sugar in an 11″ skillet over medium heat. Shake skillet to evenly distribute sugar over bottom of skillet. When sugar begins to melt (clear liquid will form around edges), shake pan as needed to keep sugar evenly covering the bottom of the skillet. When sugar in center of pan begins to turn golden (this will take about 6 minutes), stir with a wooden spoon just often enough to maintain an even color, shaking pan and allowing sugar to continue to melt between stirrings. When sugar is completely melted and amber in color, quickly spoon about 1 Tbsp. syrup into each of 6 (6-oz.) custard cups, tilting to coat bottoms evenly. Set cups in a 13″ x 9″ pan.

Mash bananas slightly with a fork to measure ¾ cup. Place banana in blender; add remaining ½ cup sugar, vanilla bean paste, and half-and-half. Process 5 seconds or just until smooth. Add eggs; process 5 seconds or just until thoroughly blended, but not foamy. Be sure not to overprocess the eggs. Pour custard evenly into prepared cups. Add hot water to pan to depth of 1″.

Bake, uncovered, at 325° for 40 minutes or until custards are set and a knife inserted near center comes out clean.

Remove cups from water bath, and cool completely on a wire rack. Cover and chill at least 8 hours. Run a paring knife around edge of each cup to loosen custards, and invert onto a serving platter, letting melted caramel drizzle down sides of custards. Top each dessert with a walnut half. **Yield: 6 servings.**

Tip: It's easiest if you place the pan containing filled custard cups on oven rack before adding hot water. Wear rubber gloves to easily remove cups from water after baking.

Chile Caribe Brownies

Although these slick brownies harbor spicy red pepper, chocolate and a hint of cinnamon tame the fire.

Prep: 5 min.   Cook: 31 min.

1   to 1½ tsp. chile caribe pepper flakes or crushed red pepper flakes (we tested with Penzeys)*
1   (19.5-oz.) package fudge brownie mix (we tested with Pillsbury)
1½   tsp. ground cinnamon
2   large eggs
½   cup canola oil
¼   cup water
2   cups dark chocolate morsels, divided (we tested with Nestlé Chocolatier)
3   Tbsp. unsalted butter, cut into small pieces
2   Tbsp. heavy whipping cream
Chile caribe pepper flakes (optional)

   Grind 1 to 1½ tsp. pepper flakes with a mortar and pestle or spice grinder until pieces are small. Combine brownie mix, ground pepper flakes, and cinnamon in a medium bowl; whisk until well blended. Stir in eggs, oil, and water until blended. Add ¾ cup chocolate morsels to batter; spoon batter into a lightly greased 13" x 9" pan. Bake at 350° for 28 to 31 minutes. Cool completely in pan on a wire rack.

   Place 1 cup chocolate morsels and butter in a large glass bowl. Microwave at HIGH 1 minute or until melted; stir in whipping cream. Pour mixture over cooled brownies, spreading to form a thin even layer. Place remaining ¼ cup chocolate morsels in a 1-cup glass measuring cup, and microwave at HIGH 30 seconds or until melted. Pour melted chocolate in a zip-top plastic freezer bag; snip a tiny hole in 1 corner of bag. Pipe a zigzag drizzle over iced brownies; sprinkle lightly with chile caribe flakes, if desired. Refrigerate brownies for easy cutting. **Yield: 20 brownies.**

*Caribe red pepper flakes are typically medium heat, but not overwhelming. Find them on the spice aisle or order a jar from www.penzeys.com or www.thespicehouse.com.

Chile Caribe Brownies

Vanilla-Banana-Caramel Flan

Double Chocolate Surprise Cupcakes

Dark Chocolate Truffles with Fleur de Sel

Double Chocolate Surprise Cupcakes

Prep: 14 min.   Cook: 18 min.   Other: 5 min.

1   cup butter, softened
1   cup granulated sugar
½   cup firmly packed brown sugar
4   large eggs
6   (1-oz.) unsweetened chocolate squares, melted
     and cooled
1   tsp. vanilla extract
2   cups all-purpose flour
1   tsp. baking soda
¼   tsp. salt
1   cup buttermilk
1   (7-oz.) jar marshmallow crème
1   (15.5-oz.) can triple chocolate fudge chip frosting
     (we tested with Betty Crocker)
Garnishes: assorted Christmas sprinkles and candies*

Beat butter at medium speed with an electric mixer until fluffy; gradually add sugars, beating well. Add eggs, 1 at a time, beating after each addition. Add melted chocolate and vanilla, mixing well.

Combine flour, baking soda, and salt; add to batter alternately with buttermilk, beginning and ending with flour. Mix at low speed after each addition until blended.

Spoon batter into paper-lined standard muffin pans, filling each cup full. Bake at 350° for 15 to 18 minutes or until a wooden pick inserted in center comes out clean. Cool 5 minutes in pans. Remove from pans, and cool completely on a wire rack.

Take a plug out of center top of each cupcake, going pretty deep but not quite to the bottom of each cake. (Reserve these little cupcake pieces.)

Spoon marshmallow crème into a zip-top freezer bag; seal bag, and cut a hole (about ½") in 1 corner. Squirt crème into hole of each cupcake. Replace just the top portion of each cupcake piece to regain a smooth top. Gently frost cupcakes; decorate as desired. **Yield: 20 cupcakes.**

*We tested with peppermint candies and a Winter Wonderland decorating kit from Williams-Sonoma.

Dark Chocolate Truffles with Fleur de Sel

These sinfully rich truffles earned our Test Kitchens highest rating. For information on fleur de sel, see page 165.

Prep: 30 min. Cook: 12 min. Other: 3 hr.

8	oz. bittersweet chocolate, chopped
¼	cup sugar
1	Tbsp. water
⅔	cup heavy whipping cream
¼	tsp. fleur de sel or coarse sea salt
½	cup Dutch process cocoa, sifted
12	oz. bittersweet chocolate, broken

Fleur de sel or coarse sea salt to taste

Microwave 8 oz. chocolate in a glass bowl at HIGH 1 minute or until melted.

Combine sugar and water in a small heavy saucepan; cook over medium heat until sugar dissolves, stirring gently. Continue to simmer, without stirring, about 7 minutes or until syrup is golden, brushing down sides of pan with a pastry brush dipped in water; remove pan from heat. Carefully add cream (mixture will bubble). Return pan to low heat, and simmer, stirring until smooth. Stir in ¼ tsp. fleur de sel. Remove from heat. Add cream mixture to melted chocolate; stir until smooth, and let cool. Cover and chill 3 hours or until firm.

Place cocoa in a bowl. Shape chocolate mixture into 1" balls (we used a 1" ice cream scoop); roll in cocoa. Place truffle balls on a baking sheet; chill until firm.

Place 12 oz. chocolate in top of a double boiler over simmering water until a thermometer inserted into chocolate registers 115°.* Remove top insert; working quickly, dip truffles in melted chocolate, coating completely. Lift out truffles with a small fork, letting excess chocolate drip off. Tilt double boiler insert, if needed, to make dipping and coating easier. Return top insert to heat every few minutes to keep chocolate at 115°. Transfer truffles to parchment paper. Sprinkle truffles lightly with additional fleur de sel. Let stand until chocolate coating is set. **Yield: about 2 dozen.**

*It's important to keep the saucepan of melted chocolate at 115° for coating the truffles. As your guide, use a candy or digital thermometer, easily found at your local cook store. Once this chocolate coating hardens on the candy, it will lend a nice crunch when you bite into it.

Vanilla Spice Pistachio Cheesecake

Vanilla, cardamom, and white chocolate unite in this creamy holiday dessert.

Prep: 21 min. Cook: 1 hr., 30 min. Other: 8 hr., 10 min.

½	(10-oz.) package shortbread cookies (we tested with Lorna Doone)
½	cup unsalted pistachio nuts
¼	cup sugar
¼	cup butter, melted
3	(8-oz.) packages cream cheese, softened
1¼	cups sugar
1	tsp. ground cardamom
2¾	cups sour cream, divided
1	Tbsp. all-purpose flour
1	Tbsp. vanilla bean paste or vanilla extract
4	large eggs
5	oz. white chocolate, chopped

Garnish: additional unsalted pistachio nuts

Place first 3 ingredients in a food processor; process until finely ground. Stir in butter. Press cookie crumb mixture into bottom of an ungreased 9" springform pan. Bake at 350° for 15 minutes.

Meanwhile, beat cream cheese, 1¼ cups sugar, and cardamom at medium speed with an electric mixer until smooth. Add 1½ cups sour cream, flour, and vanilla bean paste; beat until blended. Add eggs, 1 at a time, beating just until yellow disappears. Pour batter into baked crust.

Bake at 300° for 1 hour and 15 minutes or until almost set. Immediately run a knife around edge of pan, releasing sides. Let cool on a wire rack 10 minutes.

Meanwhile, place white chocolate in a microwave-safe bowl; microwave at HIGH for 1 minute or until chocolate is soft. Stir until smooth. Whisk in remaining 1¼ cups sour cream. Spread white chocolate mixture over warm cheesecake. Let cool completely in pan on wire rack. Cover and chill 8 hours. Remove sides of pan. Garnish cheesecake, if desired. **Yield: 12 servings.**

Vanilla Sugar

This recipe provides a great way to enjoy the essence of a vanilla bean. Substitute this vanilla-flecked sugar for regular granulated sugar to add richness to just about anything you bake.

Prep: 5 min.

2   vanilla bean pods (seeds already scraped for another recipe)
3   cups sugar

Cut each vanilla bean pod into 4 pieces, splaying open each piece to expose any remaining vanilla seeds and essence. Place in a canister or a plastic container with sugar, and stir gently. Cover canister, and store in a cool, dry place. Discard pod pieces after 1 month. **Yield: 3 cups.**

gift idea • make ahead
Vanilla Bean Oil

Vanilla bean oil is very delicate in flavor and quite versatile— use it to flavor salads, seafood, or poultry; or drizzle it over sweet potatoes before roasting.

Prep: 3 min. Cook: 3 min. Other: 24 hr.

2   cups canola oil
2   vanilla beans, split lengthwise

Pour oil into a saucepan. Using the tip of a small sharp knife, scrape vanilla bean seeds into oil; add vanilla bean pods to pan. Bring oil just to a simmer over medium-low heat. Remove from heat; let cool completely.

Pour oil into a clean jar with a tight fitting lid; cover and chill 24 hours. Discard vanilla bean pods. Store oil in refrigerator up to 1 month. Before each use, let oil stand at room temperature at least 30 minutes. **Yield: 2 cups.**

Note: Here's our favorite recommendation for Vanilla Bean Oil. Lightly drizzle mixed baby greens with the oil; squeeze a lemon half over greens, sprinkle with salt, and gently toss. Add a handful of fresh or dried blueberries and toasted almonds, if desired.

Candy Cane Soufflés

These soufflés are impressive when served straight from the oven. The crème anglaise can be prepared a day ahead and then chilled.

Prep: 7 min. Cook: 30 min.

1   cup hard peppermint candies (about 35 candies)
Butter
2   Tbsp. sugar
4   eggs yolks
2   Tbsp. sugar
4   Tbsp. butter
6   oz. dark chocolate, chopped (we tested with Ghirardelli)
6   Tbsp. all-purpose flour
1   cup milk
1   cup heavy whipping cream
2   tsp. vanilla extract
1   tsp. peppermint extract
7   egg whites
⅛   tsp. cream of tartar
Very Vanilla Crème Anglaise
Garnish: small candy canes

Place 1 cup candies in a food processor; process until candies are ground. Set aside.

Lightly butter bottoms and sides of 6 (8-oz.) individual soufflé ramekins. Sprinkle 2 Tbsp. sugar evenly into ramekins, tilting ramekins to coat sides. Place ramekins on a baking sheet; set aside.

Whisk together 4 egg yolks and 2 Tbsp. sugar in a large bowl. Melt 4 Tbsp. butter and chocolate in a small heavy saucepan over medium-low heat. Whisk in flour; cook 1 minute. Gradually whisk in milk and cream; cook, stirring constantly, 3 minutes or until thickened. Remove from heat; add a small amount of chocolate mixture to egg yolk mixture, whisking constantly. Continue adding chocolate mixture in small amounts, whisking constantly until thoroughly blended. Stir in reserved candies, vanilla, and peppermint extract.

Beat egg whites and cream of tartar at high speed with an electric mixer until stiff peaks form. Fold into peppermint mixture. Pour into prepared soufflé dishes. Bake at 375° for 24 minutes or until puffed and slightly browned on top. Serve immediately with Very Vanilla Crème Anglaise. Garnish, if desired. **Yield: 6 servings.**

Very Vanilla Crème Anglaise:

Prep: 2 min.   Cook: 10 min.

3 egg yolks
2 Tbsp. sugar
½ vanilla bean or 1½ tsp. vanilla extract
1 cup heavy whipping cream

Whisk egg yolks and sugar in a bowl until blended.
Split vanilla bean piece lengthwise; scrape seeds into cream using knife blade. Bring cream and vanilla bean seeds just to a boil in a medium-size heavy saucepan; reduce heat, and simmer 4 minutes. Stir one-fourth of hot milk mixture gradually into yolks; add yolk mixture to remaining milk mixture, stirring constantly. Cook over medium-low heat, stirring constantly, 6 minutes or until custard reaches 160° and coats the back of a spoon. Remove from heat, and set aside to cool. Store in refrigerator. **Yield: 1 cup.**

editor's favorite • quick & easy
Cacao and Milk Chocolate Scones

This recipe is like a sweet version of drop biscuits. Find cacao nibs packaged at gourmet food stores.

Prep: 12 min.   Cook: 18 min.

3 cups all-purpose flour
⅔ cup sugar
1 Tbsp. baking powder
½ tsp. salt
¾ cup cold unsalted butter, cut into pieces
1 cup milk chocolate morsels or chopped milk
   chocolate bar (we tested with Hershey's)
½ cup cacao nibs or chopped toasted pecans
1 large egg
1 cup whipping cream
2 tsp. vanilla extract
Whipping cream (optional)
Coarse or granulated sugar (optional)

Stir together first 4 ingredients in a large bowl; cut in butter with a pastry blender until crumbly. Stir in chocolate morsels and cacao nibs.
Whisk together egg, 1 cup whipping cream, and vanilla; add to flour mixture, stirring with a fork just until dry ingredients are moistened and mixture forms a shaggy dough. Using a ⅓-cup measuring cup, scoop dough into mounds onto parchment paper-lined baking sheets. Brush

Cacao and Milk Chocolate Scones

1. Cacao nibs are unsweetened, roasted, and crushed cacao beans. They give these scones a toasty, bittersweet flavor.
2. Brush scones with cream; sprinkle with sugar for a crunchy finish.

scones with additional cream, and sprinkle with sugar, if desired.
Bake at 425° for 18 minutes or until golden. Serve warm. **Yield: 14 scones.**

Candied Orange Truffle Tart

Candied Orange Truffle Tart

Buy a fresh jar of curry powder and premium chocolate for this fudgy dessert. You'll be pleasantly surprised that curry permeates the trufflelike filling, candied orange topping, and yummy syrup. A sharp knife will cut easily through the decorated tart.

Prep: 12 min. Cook: 1 hr. Other: 4 hr.

1⅔	cups all-purpose flour
2	Tbsp. sugar
¼	tsp. salt
10	Tbsp. unsalted butter, chilled and cut into ½" pieces
2	to 3 Tbsp. ice water
1	large egg yolk
1	tsp. vanilla extract
1	cup whipping cream
2	Tbsp. sugar
2½	Tbsp. frozen orange juice concentrate
2½	tsp. curry powder (optional)
12	oz. dark chocolate, finely chopped (we tested with Ghirardelli Intense Dark 72% Cacao)
1	cup water
1	cup sugar
½	tsp. curry powder (optional)
2	navel oranges, thinly sliced

Pulse first 3 ingredients in a food processor 3 or 4 times or until combined. Add butter, and pulse 5 or 6 times or until crumbly. With processor running, gradually add 2 Tbsp. water, egg yolk, and vanilla; process until dough forms a ball and leaves sides of bowl, adding more water if necessary. Cover and chill 1½ hours.

Roll dough to a 12" circle on a lightly floured surface. Fit pastry in a 9" tart pan with removable bottom. Trim off excess pastry, allowing edges to overhang ½"; fold in overhang against inside edge of pan to form double-thick sides. Pierce bottom of pastry with a fork; freeze 20 minutes. Bake at 375° for 30 minutes or until lightly browned. Cool completely in pan on a wire rack.

Whisk together whipping cream and next 3 ingredients in a medium saucepan. Bring to a simmer over medium-low heat. Add chocolate, and whisk until smooth. Pour filling into baked crust. Refrigerate 2 hours or until firm.

Whisk together 1 cup water, 1 cup sugar, and, if desired, ½ tsp. curry powder in a large heavy skillet. Bring to a simmer over medium-high heat, stirring until sugar dissolves. Add orange slices to pan. Reduce heat to medium-low; simmer 25 to 30 minutes, turning slices occasionally, or until orange slices are translucent. Remove pan from heat; allow orange slices to cool in syrup.

Arrange orange slices on top of tart before serving. Spoon remaining syrup over each serving. **Yield: 10 to 12 servings.**

Fix It Faster: Omit the homemade crust (first 7 ingredients), and use ½ of a 15-oz. package of refrigerated piecrusts. Unroll piecrust and fit into pan. Prick with a fork. Bake at 375° for 18 minutes or until golden. Cool completely and proceed with filling.

gift idea • make ahead
Speckled Vanilla-Hazelnut Brittle

Banana chips add texture in this vanilla bean-freckled brittle. Your kitchen will smell like Bananas Foster as they're stirred into the hot candy.

Prep: 7 min. Cook: 29 min.

1½	cups hazelnuts with skins
1¾	cups granulated sugar
½	cup light corn syrup
¼	tsp. salt
½	cup hot water
½	cup dried banana chips
3	Tbsp. butter, melted
½	tsp. baking soda
1	Tbsp. vanilla bean paste

Spread hazelnuts in a single layer on a 15" x 10" jelly-roll pan. Bake at 350° for 5 to 10 minutes or until skins begin to split. Transfer warm nuts to a colander; using a towel, rub briskly to remove skins. Coarsely chop nuts.

Cook sugar and next 3 ingredients in a large heavy saucepan over medium heat, stirring constantly, until mixture starts to boil. Boil without stirring until a candy thermometer registers 290°. Carefully stir in nuts using a clean spoon. Remove from heat, and stir in banana chips and remaining ingredients. (Baking soda will cause candy to foam.) When foaming subsides, quickly pour candy onto a buttered baking sheet. Pour as thinly as possible without spreading. After 2 to 3 minutes, use 2 buttered forks to stretch and pull brittle as fast as possible before brittle starts to break. Cool completely, and break into irregular size pieces. Store in an airtight container. **Yield: about 1¾ lb.**

Blackened Sea Scallops over Stone-Ground Grits with Vanilla Beurre Blanc

Plump scallops coated with a spicy cornmeal crust are blackened in a hot skillet. What makes this dish unique is the delicate vanilla sauce that's dribbled over the scallops and creamy grits.

Prep: 22 min. Cook: 24 min.

3½   cups chicken broth
2   Tbsp. yellow cornmeal
1   tsp. paprika
¼   tsp. salt
¼   tsp. garlic powder
¼   tsp. freshly ground black pepper
¼   tsp. ground red pepper
¼   tsp. dried oregano
¼   tsp. dried thyme
¾   cup uncooked stone-ground grits
½   cup freshly grated Parmesan cheese
2   Tbsp. butter
Vanilla Beurre Blanc
12   large sea scallops
1   Tbsp. olive oil
Fresh chives, cut into pieces

Blackened Sea Scallops over Stone-Ground Grits with Vanilla Beurre Blanc

Bring chicken broth to a boil in a 3-qt. saucepan. Meanwhile, combine cornmeal and next 7 ingredients in a zip-top plastic bag. Set aside.

Stir grits into broth, whisking constantly. Cover and cook 10 minutes or until desired thickness, stirring occasionally. Stir in Parmesan cheese and 2 Tbsp. butter. Remove from heat; cover to keep warm.

Meanwhile, prepare Vanilla Beurre Blanc.

Pat scallops dry with paper towels. Place scallops in zip-top plastic freezer bag with cornmeal mixture; seal bag, and toss to coat well.

Heat oil in a large skillet over medium-high heat until very hot. Place scallops in hot skillet, and cook 3 minutes. Turn scallops, reduce heat to medium, and cook 3 more minutes or just until done.

Just before serving, reheat grits over medium-low heat, adding a little chicken broth, if needed. Spoon grits onto serving plates. Arrange scallops on grits; drizzle with Vanilla Beurre Blanc. Sprinkle with chives. Serve hot. **Yield: 4 servings.**

Vanilla Beurre Blanc:

Prep: 2 min. Cook: 12 min.

2   Tbsp. minced shallot
¼   cup clam juice
¼   cup whipping cream
2   tsp. vanilla bean paste or vanilla extract
¾   cup cold butter, cut into 1 Tbsp. pieces
1   Tbsp. vanilla vodka
Pinch of salt

Combine shallot and clam juice in a 10" skillet; bring to a boil over medium-high heat. Add cream. Cook for 3 minutes or until liquid is almost evaporated. Stir in vanilla bean paste.

Reduce heat to low, and whisk in butter, 1 Tbsp. at a time, whisking after each addition, until butter melts. Swirl pan, as necessary after each addition of butter, removing pan from heat to prevent butter from browning. Whisk in vodka and salt. Serve hot. **Yield: ⅔ cup.**

Vanilla is a subtle and delightful success in these savory entrées.

Mushroom Bread Pudding with Vanilla Lobster Sauce

This is an intriguing meatless entrée with a velvety seafood sauce that whispers of vanilla.

Prep: 15 min.   Cook: 54 min.   Other: 30 min.

¼   cup butter
1   (3.5-oz.) package fresh shiitake mushrooms, sliced
1   cup thinly sliced leeks
½   cup thinly sliced celery
8   cups torn crusty white bread (not sandwich bread)
1½ cups whipping cream
¼   cup clam juice
4   large eggs, lightly beaten
½   tsp. vanilla extract
½   tsp. salt
⅛   tsp. ground nutmeg
Dash of ground white pepper
Vanilla Lobster Sauce
Garnish: fresh tarragon

Melt butter in a large skillet over medium heat. Add mushrooms, leeks, and celery; sauté 7 to 8 minutes or until tender. Combine sautéed vegetables and bread in a large bowl; toss well.

Combine whipping cream and next 6 ingredients; pour over bread mixture, and toss well. Cover and let soak in refrigerator 30 minutes.

Meanwhile, prepare Vanilla Lobster Sauce.

Pour bread pudding mixture into a buttered 11" x 7" baking dish. Bake, uncovered, at 350° for 45 minutes or until set and lightly browned. Serve Vanilla Lobster Sauce over bread pudding. Garnish each serving, if desired. **Yield: 6 servings.**

Vanilla Lobster Sauce:

Prep: 19 min.   Cook: 1 hr., 6 min.

2   (8-oz.) fresh or frozen lobster tails, thawed
1   Tbsp. olive oil
1   cup chopped onion
2   garlic cloves, pressed
½   tsp. double-concentrated tomato paste
¼   cup Cognac or brandy
3   cups water
2   Tbsp. butter
2½ Tbsp. all-purpose flour
1   cup whipping cream
½   vanilla bean, split lengthwise and seeds removed and reserved*
¼   tsp. salt
2   tsp. minced fresh tarragon

Cook lobster tails in boiling salted water to cover 3 minutes or until opaque in center; drain and cool slightly. Using kitchen shears or a sharp knife, split tails lengthwise. Remove meat, and cut into ½" pieces. Set meat aside, and reserve shells.

Heat oil in a large saucepan over medium-high heat. Add onion and garlic; sauté 4 minutes or until tender. Add tomato paste; cook 1 minute. Remove pan from heat; stir in Cognac. Add water and reserved lobster shells; bring to a boil. Cover, reduce heat, and simmer 30 minutes. Pour broth through a wire-mesh strainer into a large measuring cup or bowl, discarding shells.

Melt butter in a large skillet over medium heat; whisk in flour until smooth. Cook 1 minute, whisking constantly. Gradually whisk in lobster stock, whipping cream, and vanilla bean seeds; bring to a boil. Reduce heat, and simmer 15 minutes or until sauce reduces to 2 cups. Stir in salt, tarragon, and chopped lobster meat. Keep warm until ready to serve. **Yield: 3 cups.**

*Substitute ½ tsp. vanilla extract, if desired.

Note: Here's a tip to make the most of your vanilla bean flavor—measure the whipping cream for this sauce and gently scrape vanilla bean seeds into the whipping cream using the tip of a paring knife. Plop the vanilla bean pod into the whipping cream and let stand while preparing the lobster stock. Remove pod before pouring cream and seeds into stock.

HOLIDAY *Baking*

For many folks baking is one of the most anticipated activities during the yuletide season. This collection of classics has something sweet for every age.

make ahead
Gingerbread Girls

These firm, crisp, delicious cookies are perfect for topping off a stocking, decorating a mantel, or forming a centerpiece.

Prep: 1 hr., 20 min.   Cook: 14 min. per batch   Other: 2 hr.

¼   cup granulated sugar
¼   cup firmly packed dark brown sugar
½   cup molasses
2   tsp. ground ginger
1   tsp. ground allspice
1   tsp. ground cinnamon
1   tsp. ground cloves
2   tsp. baking soda
½   cup unsalted butter, cut into pieces
1   large egg, lightly beaten
3   cups all-purpose flour
¼   tsp. salt
½   cup raisins (optional)
¼   cup red cinnamon candies (optional)
Royal Icing (see next page)
Candy decorations* (optional)

Combine first 7 ingredients in a 3-qt. saucepan. Bring to a boil over medium heat, stirring occasionally. Remove pan from heat; stir in baking soda. Transfer to a mixing bowl. Add butter and egg, beating at medium speed with an electric mixer until smooth. Gradually stir in flour and salt, beating just until blended.

Shape dough into a ball, and divide in half. Flatten each half into a round disk; wrap each in plastic wrap, and chill at least 1 hour or until firm.

Line several large baking sheets with parchment paper. Roll out dough, 1 section at a time, to ¼" thickness on a floured surface. Cut into gingerbread girl shapes (we used a 5½" cookie cutter from www.rochowcutters.com). Reroll

1. Fill a zip-top plastic freezer bag with icing, snip a small hole in 1 corner of bag, and first outline desired patterns on each cookie.
2. After outlining, fill in with same icing. Allow to dry at least 1 hour before handling cookies.

trimmings to make additional cookies. Place cutouts ½" apart on prepared baking sheets.

Bake cutouts plain, or press raisins and cinnamon candies in each gingerbread girl for eyes, nose, mouth, and buttons, if desired.

Bake at 325° for 14 minutes or until cookies are puffed and slightly darker around edges. Cool 1 minute on baking sheets; remove to wire racks to cool completely.

Decorate cookies with Royal Icing by first outlining desired patterns for each cookie. Then fill in with additional icing, letting icing flow into outlined area. Apply candy decorations, if desired. Let icing harden at least 1 hour. **Yield: 16 cookies.**

*We tested with Williams-Sonoma Winter Wonderland Decorating Kit.

Royal Icing:

Prep: 20 min.

1 (16-oz.) package powdered sugar
3 Tbsp. meringue powder
½ cup lukewarm water
Paste food coloring

Combine first 3 ingredients in a large bowl; beat at medium speed with an electric mixer 5 to 6 minutes or until icing is firm enough to pipe, but still of spreading consistency, adding a few drops of additional water if necessary for right consistency. Divide icing into small bowls, and tint each by dipping a wooden pick into paste coloring and stirring it into icing until desired color is reached. Icing dries quickly; keep it covered at all times.

Spoon icing into zip-top plastic freezer bags, and snip a small hole in 1 corner of each bag. **Yield: 3⅔ cups.**

Christmas Pannetone

We chose to bake this European holiday bread in a springform pan instead of the traditional cylindrical-shaped pan.

Prep: 12 min.   Cook: 45 min.   Other: 4 hr.

⅔ cup currants
⅔ cup diced dried apricots
⅔ cup raisins
¼ cup bourbon
1 (.25-oz.) package active dry yeast
½ cup warm milk (100° to 110°)
1 cup all-purpose flour
½ cup unsalted butter, softened
½ cup granulated sugar
½ tsp. salt
3 Tbsp. grated orange rind
2 tsp. vanilla extract
3 cups all-purpose flour
4 large eggs, lightly beaten
2 Tbsp. unsalted butter, melted
Powdered sugar (optional)
Mascarpone Cream

Combine currants, apricots, raisins, and bourbon in a small bowl. Let stand 1 hour or up to 4 hours.

Combine yeast and milk in a medium bowl; whisk until smooth. Stir in 1 cup flour until well blended; cover and let rise 30 minutes.

Combine ½ cup butter, sugar, and salt in a bowl; beat at medium speed with an electric mixer 3 to 5 minutes or until light and fluffy. Add orange rind and vanilla; beat 2 minutes. Add 3 cups flour alternately with eggs, beginning and ending with flour. Stir in yeast mixture. Turn out dough onto a floured surface, and knead until smooth while gradually folding in fruit mixture (8 to 10 minutes). Place dough in a buttered bowl, turning to butter the top. Cover with plastic wrap, and let rise in warm place (85°), free from drafts, 1½ hours or until doubled in bulk.

Butter a 10" springform pan. Place dough in pan, pressing to evenly fill pan. Cover with plastic wrap, and let rise 1 hour, or until dough reaches top of pan. Bake at 350° for 45 minutes or until a wooden pick inserted in center comes out clean, shielding with foil after 30 minutes to prevent excessive browning. Remove from oven, and brush with 2 tablespoons melted butter. Cool in pan on a wire rack 5 minutes. Remove sides of pan, and allow bread to cool. Dust with powdered sugar, if desired. Serve with Mascarpone Cream. **Yield: 10 to 12 servings.**

Mascarpone Cream:

Prep: 2 min.

1 (8-oz.) container mascarpone cheese
2 Tbsp. amaretto liqueur
1 Tbsp. powdered sugar

Combine all ingredients in a small bowl, stirring well to blend. Store in refrigerator. **Yield: about 1½ cups.**

Candy Bar Brown Sugar Cakes

Prep: 22 min.   Cook: 25 min.   Other: 10 min.

¾ cup butter, softened
⅓ cup shortening
1½ cups firmly packed light brown sugar
¾ cup granulated sugar
3 large eggs
2¼ cups all-purpose flour
1 tsp. baking powder
½ tsp. salt
¾ cup milk
2 tsp. vanilla extract
¾ cup toffee bits
3 (2.7-oz.) chocolate-coated caramel-peanut nougat bars, coarsely chopped
Powdered sugar

Beat butter and shortening at medium speed with an electric mixer 2 minutes or until creamy. Gradually add brown and granulated sugars, beating until light and fluffy. Add eggs, 1 at a time, beating just until blended.

Combine flour, baking powder, and salt. Add to butter mixture alternately with milk, beginning and ending with dry ingredients. Stir in vanilla and toffee bits.

Spoon batter into 2 greased and floured Bundtlette pans, filling each cup ⅔ full. Sprinkle with chopped nougat bars, pressing candy gently into batter.

Bake at 325° for 25 minutes or until a wooden pick inserted in center comes out clean. Cool in pans 10 minutes. Remove from pans to cool on wire racks. Sprinkle with powdered sugar before serving. **Yield: 1 dozen.**

Note: See page 138 for more about Bundtlette pans.

Big Crunchy Sugar Cookies

editor's favorite • gift idea
Big Crunchy Sugar Cookies

Sparkling sugar cookies are holiday classics. These goodies, which earn their name from a coating of coarse sugar, received our Test Kitchens highest rating.

Prep: 20 min.   Cook: 15 min.   Other: 2 hr.

1	cup unsalted butter, softened
1	cup granulated sugar
1	large egg
1½	tsp. vanilla extract
2	cups all-purpose flour
½	tsp. baking powder
¼	tsp. salt

Assorted coarse decorator sugars

Beat butter at medium speed with an electric mixer until creamy. Gradually add 1 cup sugar, beating until smooth. Add egg and vanilla, beating until blended.

Combine flour, baking powder, and salt; gradually add to butter mixture, beating just until blended. Shape dough into a ball; cover and chill 2 hours.

Divide dough into 3 portions. Work with 1 portion of dough at a time, storing remaining dough in refrigerator. Shape dough into 1½" balls; roll each ball in decorator sugar. Place 2" apart on parchment-lined baking sheets. Gently press and flatten each ball of dough to ¾" thickness. Bake at 375° 13 to 15 minutes or until edges of cookies are lightly browned. Cool 5 minutes on baking sheets; remove to wire racks to cool. **Yield: 18 cookies.**

Part of the charm of these cookies is that the dough balls are heavily sugar coated. Coarse sugar comes in a variety of colors. Pick your favorite solids, and then mix complementary sugars.

Classic Fruitcake Loaves

For a nonalcoholic version, use root beer instead of brandy as the soaking liquid.

Prep: 45 min.   Cook: 2 hr., 30 min.

1½   cups unsalted butter, softened
¾   cup granulated sugar
¾   cup firmly packed dark brown sugar
¼   cup molasses
1   Tbsp. orange extract
3   cups all-purpose flour
1   tsp. ground cinnamon
1   tsp. ground allspice
½   tsp. ground cloves
7   large eggs, lightly beaten
3½   cups chopped candied pineapple
1   (8-oz.) container red candied cherries, chopped
1   (8-oz.) container green candied cherries, chopped
3   cups pecan halves, coarsely chopped and toasted
1   cup walnut halves, coarsely chopped and toasted
1   cup raisins
½   cup golden raisins
½   cup all-purpose flour
Garnishes: additional candied cherries and pecan halves
3   Tbsp. brandy (optional)
Additional brandy (optional)

Beat butter at medium speed with a heavy-duty electric stand mixer until creamy; gradually add sugars, beating well. Add molasses and orange extract, beating well. Combine flour and next 3 ingredients. Add to butter mixture alternately with beaten eggs, beginning and ending with flour mixture. Beat well after each addition.

Combine candied pineapple, chopped cherries, and next 4 ingredients in a large bowl; sprinkle with ½ cup flour, stirring to coat well. Stir fruit into batter. Spoon batter into 3 heavily greased and floured 8½" x 4½" loaf pans. Arrange additional cherries and pecans on top of batter, if desired.

Bake at 250° for 2½ hours or until a wooden pick inserted in center of loaves comes out clean. Brush each loaf with 1 Tbsp. brandy, if desired. Let cool completely on a wire rack. If desired, wrap loaves in brandy-soaked cheesecloth. Store in an airtight container in a cool place up to 3 weeks. Pour a small amount of brandy evenly over loaves each week, if desired. **Yield: 3 loaves.**

Glazed Cranberry-Nut Tea Bread

You'll want to make several loaves of this orange-scented quick bread—some to enjoy after meals and others to wrap and share with friends.

Prep: 12 min.   Cook: 58 min.   Other: 10 min.

½   cup unsalted butter, softened
1   cup sugar
1   large egg
2   cups all-purpose flour
1½   tsp. baking powder
1   tsp. salt
½   tsp. baking soda
½   cup buttermilk
½   cup orange juice
¾   cup coarsely chopped pecans, toasted
¾   cup sweetened dried cranberries
2   tsp. grated orange rind
Glaze (optional)

Beat butter and sugar in a large mixing bowl at medium speed with an electric mixer until fluffy. Add egg, beating until blended.

Combine flour and next 3 ingredients; add to butter mixture alternately with buttermilk and orange juice, beginning and ending with flour mixture. Stir in pecans, cranberries, and orange rind. Pour batter into a greased and floured 9" x 5" loaf pan.

Bake at 350° for 56 to 58 minutes or until a wooden pick inserted in center comes out clean. Cool in pan 10 minutes. Remove from pan. If desired, poke holes in loaf using a wooden pick, and spoon Glaze over warm loaf. Cool completely on a wire rack. **Yield: 1 loaf.**

Glaze:

Prep: 5 min.

½   cup powdered sugar
1   tsp. grated orange rind
2   Tbsp. freshly squeezed orange juice

Combine all ingredients in a small bowl, stirring with a whisk until smooth. **Yield: ¼ cup.**

Cranberry
Upside-Down Cake

Cranberry Upside-Down Cake

Shiny glazed cranberries give a tangy new twist to this classic homestyle dessert.

Prep: 16 min.   Cook: 1 hr.   Other: 10 min.

½	cup butter
3	Tbsp. amaretto liqueur
1¼	cups firmly packed brown sugar
24	whole natural almonds, lightly toasted
2¼	cups fresh or frozen cranberries
¾	cup coarsely chopped natural almonds, toasted
1½	cups all-purpose flour
2	tsp. baking powder
½	cup butter, softened
1	cup granulated sugar
3	large eggs
½	cup milk
1	Tbsp. vanilla extract
1	tsp. almond extract

Melt ½ cup butter in a lightly greased 10" cast-iron skillet over low heat. Stir amaretto into melted butter; sprinkle brown sugar into skillet. Remove from heat.

Arrange whole almonds around edge of skillet. Sprinkle cranberries and chopped almonds over brown sugar.

Whisk together flour and baking powder in a medium bowl. Set aside. Beat softened butter at medium speed with an electric mixer until creamy; gradually add granulated sugar, beating well. Add eggs, 1 at a time, beating until blended after each addition. Add flour mixture to butter mixture, alternately with milk, beginning and ending with flour mixture. Beat at low speed until blended after each addition. Stir in extracts. Pour batter over cranberries and almonds in skillet.

Bake at 350° for 55 to 60 minutes or until a wooden pick inserted in center comes out clean. Cool in skillet on a wire rack 10 minutes. Run a knife around edges. Invert cake onto a serving plate. **Yield: 1 (10") cake.**

Whipped Cream Caramel Cake

editor's favorite • make ahead

Whipped Cream Caramel Cake

Shy away from making caramel frosting? No worries here—this is the easiest caramel frosting ever. It takes its time firming up, so there's no need to rush while frosting the layers.

Prep: 27 min.   Cook: 28 min.   Other: 1 hr., 10 min.

1   cup unsalted butter, softened
1½   cups sugar
4   large eggs
2¼   cups sifted cake flour
2   tsp. baking powder
½   tsp. salt
¾   cup milk
1   Tbsp. vanilla extract
       Whipped Cream Caramel Frosting
2   (1.4-oz.) chocolate-covered toffee candy bars,
       coarsely broken
1   (4.5-oz.) package dark chocolate-covered almonds,
       halved (we tested with Dove)

Beat butter and sugar at medium speed with an electric mixer until fluffy. Add eggs, 1 at a time, beating until blended after each addition.

Combine flour, baking powder, and salt; add to butter mixture alternately with milk, beginning and ending with flour mixture. Beat at low speed after each addition. Stir in vanilla. Pour batter into 2 greased and floured 8" round cake pans.

Bake at 350° for 26 to 28 minutes or until a wooden pick inserted in center comes out clean. Cool in pans on wire racks 10 minutes; remove from pans, and cool completely on wire racks. Wrap and chill cake layers at least 1 hour or up to 24 hours. (This step enables you to split layers with ease.)

Using a serrated knife, slice cake layers in half horizontally to make 4 layers. Place 1 layer on a cake plate. Spread with ½ cup Whipped Cream Caramel Frosting. Repeat procedure with remaining 3 layers. Frost sides and top of cake with remaining frosting. Decorate cake with broken toffee bars and chocolate-covered almonds. Store in refrigerator. **Yield: 1 (4-layer) cake.**

Whipped Cream Caramel Frosting:

Prep: 7 min.   Cook: 6 min.   Other: 1 hr.

1   cup unsalted butter
2   cups firmly packed dark brown sugar
¼   cup plus 2 Tbsp. whipping cream
2   tsp. vanilla extract
3¾   cups powdered sugar

Melt butter in a 3-qt. saucepan over medium heat. Add brown sugar; bring to a boil, stirring constantly. Stir in whipping cream and vanilla; bring to a boil. Remove from heat, and let cool 1 hour. Transfer to a mixing bowl.

Sift powdered sugar into icing. Beat at high speed with an electric mixer until creamy and spreading consistency. **Yield: 3¾ cups.**

Fix It Faster: This impressive cake also works well as a 2-layer cake if you don't want to split the layers. You'll have some frosting leftover, but that was okay with us!

Chocolate Chunk Candy Cane Cheesecake

Loaded with chocolate hunks and peppermint candies, slathered in a decadent chocolate ganache, and decorated with classic Christmas candies, this dessert is a "must-make" for the holidays.

Prep: 35 min.   Cook: 1 hr., 10 min.   Other: 9 hr., 10 min.

1½	cups chocolate wafer cookie crumbs (about 32 cookies)
¼	cup butter, melted
2	Tbsp. sugar
4	(8-oz.) packages cream cheese, softened
1	(14-oz.) can sweetened condensed milk
⅓	cup whipping cream
¼	cup sugar
2	Tbsp. all-purpose flour
2	tsp. vanilla extract
3	large eggs
1½	cups semisweet chocolate chunks
½	cup coarsely crushed hard peppermint candies (about 18 candies)
¾	cup whipping cream
1½	cups semisweet chocolate morsels

Garnishes: 65 soft peppermint sticks (5 small bags), broken, and peppermint bark

Our Best Basic Baking Tips

• You'll get optimal results when you place eggs, butter, and other dairy needed at room temperature for about 30 minutes before you begin baking. (There are exceptions, however, in which recipes may call for cold butter, ice water, etc.)

• To measure flour accurately, lightly spoon flour from the canister into a measuring cup. Fill the cup full to barely overflowing; then level the top with the edge of a knife.

• If a dough seems soft after blending and shaping, pop it in the refrigerator for 15 to 20 minutes. If dough seems soft after rolling out cookies or punching out biscuits, place baking sheet of cutouts or biscuits in refrigerator briefly before baking. This helps cookies and biscuits keep a nice shape.

• Always preheat your oven 10 minutes before baking. If your oven tends to bake hot, purchase an oven thermometer at the grocery store, and clip it in your oven. This way you can regulate the temperature so recipes bake accurately.

Tools for Gift Giving

In testing the holiday confections in this chapter, our Test Kitchens staff gave thumbs-up on these baking items and ingredients. Stock them in your holiday pantry, or consider them for gift giving.

• **Gingerbread girl cookie cutters.** We tested with a handsome 5½" cutter from www.rochowcutters.com

• **Nonstick Bundtlette pans.** We tested with both Nordic Ware® and Wilton pans. Each pan makes six 1-cup Bundtlettes.

• **Mini loaf pans.** These are available at kitchen shops, or you can use the disposable aluminum pans available at the grocery store.

• **Coarse decorating sugars.** These are available online and in cook stores in a variety of colors and jar sizes. They make a nice gift basket addition along with sugar cookie dough.

Combine first 3 ingredients; stir well. Press mixture firmly on bottom of a lightly greased 9" springform pan. Bake at 325° for 14 minutes; let cool.

Beat cream cheese at medium-high speed with an electric mixer until creamy. Gradually add sweetened condensed milk, beating just until blended. Add ⅓ cup whipping cream and next 3 ingredients, beating just until blended. Add eggs, 1 at a time, beating just until yellow disappears. Stir in chocolate chunks and crushed candies.

Pour batter into baked crust. Bake at 325° for 52 to 55 minutes or until edges are set and center is almost set. Turn off oven. Immediately run a knife around edge of pan, releasing sides. With oven door slightly open, let cheesecake stand in oven 1 hour. Remove from oven; cool completely on a wire rack. Cover and chill 8 hours. Remove sides and bottom of pan; place cheesecake on a serving plate.

Pour ¾ cup whipping cream into a microwave-safe bowl. Microwave at HIGH 1 minute or until hot. Add 1½ cups semisweet morsels; stir until chocolate melts and mixture is smooth. Pour ganache over chilled cheesecake, allowing ganache to spill over edges of cheesecake; smooth ganache with an offset spatula. Let stand 10 minutes before garnishing. Store in refrigerator. **Yield: 12 servings.**

Note: For easy cleanup, place wax paper strips under edges of cheesecake on serving plate. When you pour the ganache, it will drip onto the wax paper. Gently remove wax paper strips after the 10-minute standing time.

Chocolate Chunk Candy Cane Cheesecake

Star Pecan Pie

Star Pecan Pie

This versatile pie received our tasters' top rating. Display it whole during dinner where guests can admire its star-studded top and anticipate its gooey richness.

Prep: 18 min. Cook: 55 min.

Classic Pastry Shell and Pastry Stars
4	large eggs
1	Tbsp. whipping cream
1	cup firmly packed dark brown sugar
¾	cup light corn syrup
6	Tbsp. unsalted butter, melted
2	tsp. vanilla extract
¼	tsp. salt
1½	cups chopped pecans, lightly toasted
⅔	cup pecan halves

Prepare dough for Classic Pastry Shell and Pastry Stars. Roll three-fourths of dough to ⅛" thickness on a lightly floured surface. Place in a 9" pie plate; trim off excess pastry along edges. Fold edges under, and crimp. Place pastry in refrigerator while preparing Pastry Stars and pie filling.

Line a baking sheet with parchment paper. Roll remaining dough to ⅛" thickness on a lightly floured surface. Using a 1" star-shaped cutter, cut out 12 stars. Repeat procedure using a 1½" star-shaped cutter to cut out 5 stars. Transfer stars to prepared baking sheet. Whisk together 1 egg and cream in a small bowl. Remove pastry from refrigerator. Brush egg wash over Pastry Stars and around crimped edge of pastry.

Whisk remaining 3 eggs in a bowl. Whisk in brown sugar and next 4 ingredients; stir in chopped pecans. Pour filling into pastry shell. Arrange pecan halves around outer edge of filling. Arrange Pastry Stars on top of pie.

Bake at 350° on bottom oven rack for 50 to 55 minutes or until filling is set and pastry stars are browned. Transfer to a wire rack to cool completely. **Yield: 1 (9") pie.**

Pecan Pie with Grand Marnier: Prepare main recipe as directed above, but add 2 Tbsp. Grand Marnier to filling and substitute 1 tsp. orange extract for vanilla. Bake as directed.

Chocolate Pecan Pie: Prepare main recipe as directed above, but add 2 (1-oz.) squares unsweetened chocolate, melted, to filling along with butter. Bake as directed.

Classic Pastry Shell and Pastry Stars:

Prep: 7 min.

2	cups all-purpose flour
1	tsp. salt
¾	cup chilled shortening
5	to 6 Tbsp. ice water

Whisk together flour and salt; cut in shortening with a pastry blender until mixture is the size of peas. Sprinkle ice water, 1 Tbsp. at a time, over surface; stir with a fork until dry ingredients are moistened. Shape into a ball. **Yield: enough pastry for 1 (9") pie.**

Fix It Faster: Omit Classic Pastry recipe and use 1 (15-oz.) package refrigerated piecrusts. Unroll 1 piecrust and place in 9" pie plate. Fold edges under, and crimp. Unroll remaining piecrust and cut out stars according to recipe. Prepare pie and filling as recipe directs. Bake at 350° on bottom oven rack for 48 to 50 minutes.

Pumpkin-Caramel-Toffee Pie

Prep: 10 min. Cook: 50 min.

½	(15-oz.) package refrigerated piecrusts
¾	cup canned dulce de leche
2	large eggs
1	(15-oz.) can pumpkin
1	cup firmly packed brown sugar
2	Tbsp. all-purpose flour
1	Tbsp. vanilla extract or vanilla bean paste
½	tsp. salt
1	tsp. ground cinnamon
¾	tsp. ground ginger
¼	tsp. ground nutmeg
1	(12-oz.) can evaporated milk

Garnishes: sweetened whipped cream, toffee bits

Unroll piecrust, and fit into a 9½" deep-dish pie plate according to package directions. Fold edges under, and crimp. Spoon dollops of dulce de leche into piecrust, spreading to edges. Place prepared piecrust in refrigerator.

Whisk eggs in a medium bowl. Whisk in pumpkin and next 7 ingredients until smooth. Whisk in milk. Pour filling into prepared piecrust. Bake at 375° on bottom oven rack for 48 to 50 minutes or until pie is just set (center will still jiggle just slightly). Cool completely on a wire rack. Garnish, if desired. **Yield: 1 (9½") deep-dish pie.**

ELEGANT ENTRÉES, *Easy Sides*

*Take your pick from five impressive entrées, and then mix and match
from our selection of simple side dishes to round out the meal.*

Roast Pork with Sage and Pecan Pesto

*Be careful not to overprocess the flavorful pesto for this dish.
The finished sauce should have some texture remaining.*

Prep: 15 min. Cook: 1 hr., 31 min. Other: 12 hr., 10 min.

1	(64-oz.) bottle apple cider
¼	cup kosher salt
½	cup plus 3 Tbsp. chopped fresh sage, divided
1	(4-lb.) boneless pork loin roast
1	tsp. freshly ground pepper
2	Tbsp. olive oil

Garnishes: fresh sage, unshelled pecans
Sage and Pecan Pesto

Combine cider, salt, and ½ cup chopped sage, stirring
until salt dissolves. Place pork in an extra-large zip-top
plastic freezer bag; add cider mixture. Seal bag; chill 12
to 24 hours.

Remove pork from brine, and pat dry with paper towels.
Sprinkle pork with pepper. Heat oil in a large skillet over
medium-high heat; add pork. Cook 6 minutes or until
browned on all sides, turning pork occasionally. Place
pork on a rack in a lightly greased roasting pan. Sprinkle
remaining 3 Tbsp. sage over pork.

Bake, uncovered, at 350° for 1 hour to 1 hour and
25 minutes or until a meat thermometer inserted into
thickest part of roast registers 150°. Remove from oven;
cover and let rest 10 minutes or until thermometer
reaches 160° before slicing. Garnish platter, if desired.
Serve with Sage and Pecan Pesto. **Yield: 8 servings.**

Sage and Pecan Pesto:

Prep: 7 min.

½	cup chopped pecans, toasted
½	cup firmly packed fresh flat-leaf parsley
¼	cup firmly packed fresh sage leaves
¼	cup freshly grated Parmesan cheese
¼	cup extra virgin olive oil
1	tsp. fresh lemon juice
1	garlic clove, chopped
¼	tsp. salt

Combine all ingredients in a food processor; process
until ingredients are finely chopped. **Yield: ¾ cup.**

editor's favorite
Coffee-Glazed Ham with Red Eye Gravy

Prep: 10 min. Cook: 2 hr., 30 min. Other: 10 min.

1	(8- to 10-lb.) bone-in, fully cooked smoked ham half
2	cups firmly packed light brown sugar
2	cups freshly brewed coffee
¼	cup heavy whipping cream

Garnishes: fresh herbs, kumquats

Remove skin from ham, if present, and trim fat to
¼" thickness. Place ham in a lightly greased broiler pan.
Combine sugar and hot coffee in a medium bowl, stirring
until sugar dissolves; pour over ham.

Bake at 350° for 2½ hours or until a meat thermometer
inserted into thickest portion registers 140°, basting every
20 minutes. Transfer ham from pan to a serving platter.
Cover and keep warm. Pour drippings into a 4-cup glass
measuring cup; let stand 10 minutes. Pour off and discard
fat; stir cream into remaining drippings. Serve gravy with
ham. Garnish platter, if desired. **Yield: 10 to 12 servings.**

Sautéed Chicken with Figs in Port Wine Sauce

Adding a touch of balsamic or sherry vinegar to the sauce just before serving accents the flavor of figs and acts as a nice contrast to their sweetness. Ask your butcher to debone chicken breasts with skin if you can't find boneless portions. You can make this dish ahead, but store the chicken and sauce separately in the refrigerator. Just reheat when ready to serve.

Prep: 10 min.   Cook: 37 min.

4   boneless chicken breasts (skin on)
3   Tbsp. olive oil
2   tsp. minced fresh thyme
½   tsp. salt
¼   tsp. freshly ground black pepper
½   cup all-purpose flour
2   Tbsp. unsalted butter
1   cup dried Calimyrna figs, stemmed and quartered
⅓   cup minced shallots
½   cup Tawny port
1   cup beef broth
1   tsp. balsamic or sherry vinegar (optional)
Garnish: fresh thyme

Pat chicken dry with paper towels. Heat oil in a large nonstick skillet over medium-high heat until hot. Season chicken with thyme, salt, and pepper. Dredge in flour. Add chicken to skillet, skin side down; reduce heat to medium, and cook 16 minutes or until skin is browned. Turn and cook 5 minutes or until browned. Remove chicken from pan; keep warm. Discard pan drippings.

Melt butter in skillet over medium heat. Add figs and shallots; sauté 3 minutes or until shallots are tender. Add port; bring to a boil. Boil 1 minute; add beef broth, reduce heat, and simmer 3 minutes. Remove half of figs from skillet using a slotted spoon; keep warm with chicken. Process remaining figs and sauce in a food processor until smooth, stopping to scrape down sides as needed. Pour mixture through a wire-mesh strainer back into the skillet, discarding pulp and seeds. Return chicken and figs to sauce, and heat over medium-high heat 9 minutes or until chicken is done. Drizzle with vinegar, if desired. Cut chicken diagonally across the grain into thin strips. Serve sauce over chicken and figs. Garnish, if desired. **Yield: 4 servings.**

Rack of Lamb with Garlic-Herb Crust

*You'll hardly believe that this elegant and flavorful dish is so easy to prepare. The initial step of searing the racks in a skillet is key to locking in flavor. To save time, be sure to ask your butcher to **french** the lamb racks for you.*

Prep: 10 min.   Cook: 33 min.   Other: 10 min.

2   (8-rib) lamb rib roasts (1½ pounds each), frenched
1   tsp. salt
½   tsp. pepper
2   Tbsp. vegetable oil
½   cup fresh breadcrumbs
¼   cup minced fresh flat-leaf parsley
1   Tbsp. minced fresh rosemary
½   tsp. salt
½   tsp. pepper
4   large garlic cloves, minced
2   Tbsp. mayonnaise
2   Tbsp. Dijon mustard
Garnish: fresh rosemary

Pat lamb dry with paper towels; season with 1 tsp. salt and ½ tsp. pepper. Heat oil in a large skillet over high heat. Cook lamb in hot oil 3 to 4 minutes on each side or until browned. Place lamb on a rack in a broiler pan.

Combine breadcrumbs and next 5 ingredients in a small bowl. Combine mayonnaise and mustard in a small bowl. Brush mustard mixture over meaty top side of lamb racks; pat herb mixture evenly over mustard to adhere.

Bake at 350° for 20 to 25 minutes or until a thermometer inserted into thickest portion registers 145° (medium rare). Let stand 10 minutes. Garnish platter, if desired. Cut each rack into double chops. **Yield: 8 servings.**

Note: You'll want to ask your local butcher to french the racks of lamb for you, trimming them down to clean bones and small succulent eyes of meat that will be easy to cut apart after roasting.

editor's favorite

Rosemary Beef Tenderloin with Balsamic Peppers

Prep: 13 min.   Cook: 48 min.   Other: 10 min.

1   (5- to 5½-lb.) beef tenderloin
2   tsp. kosher salt
1½   tsp. freshly ground pepper
2   Tbsp. olive oil
3   Tbsp. minced garlic
2   Tbsp. minced fresh rosemary
     Balsamic Peppers
     Garnish: fresh rosemary sprigs

Trim fat from tenderloin. Sprinkle tenderloin all over with salt and pepper. Heat oil in a roasting pan over medium-high heat; add tenderloin. Cook 6 to 8 minutes, turning often to brown all sides. Remove tenderloin to a cutting board. Rub tenderloin with garlic and 2 Tbsp. rosemary, pressing to adhere. Return to pan. Bake, uncovered, at 400° for 40 minutes or until a meat thermometer inserted into thickest part of tenderloin registers 140° (rare) to 160° (medium). Remove tenderloin to a serving platter; let stand 10 minutes before slicing. Arrange Balsamic Peppers around tenderloin, and garnish, if desired. **Yield: 8 to 10 servings.**

Balsamic Peppers:

Prep: 15 min.   Cook: 25 min.   Other: 15 min.

2   large red bell peppers
2   large yellow bell peppers
1   red onion, cut into 8 wedges
2   Tbsp. balsamic vinegar
2   Tbsp. extra virgin olive oil
2   tsp. molasses
½   tsp. salt
⅛   tsp. freshly ground black pepper
1   Tbsp. minced fresh rosemary

Cut peppers in half lengthwise; discard seeds and membranes. Place pepper halves, skin side up, on a large aluminum foil-lined baking sheet; flatten peppers with palm of hand. Add onion to baking sheet. Broil 5½" from heat 20 to 25 minutes or until peppers are blackened. Place peppers in a zip-top plastic bag; seal, and let stand 15 minutes. Peel skin from peppers; cut pepper into strips.

Whisk together vinegar and next 4 ingredients in a medium bowl; stir in rosemary. Add pepper strips and onion to bowl; toss well. **Yield: 2¾ cups.**

Rack of Lamb with Garlic-Herb Crust

Rosemary Beef Tenderloin with Balsamic Peppers

editor's favorite • quick & easy
Blue Cheese and Black Pepper Potatoes

You'll love these spuds made luscious with blue cheese.

Prep: 2 min.   Cook: 8 min.

2   (24-oz.) packages refrigerated mashed potatoes (we tested with Bob Evans)*
4   oz. blue cheese, crumbled
¼   cup butter, cut into pieces
¼   tsp. salt
¼   tsp. freshly ground black pepper

Heat potatoes in a large saucepan over medium heat, stirring often, 6 to 8 minutes. Add blue cheese, butter, salt, and pepper, stirring just until butter is melted. **Yield: 8 to 10 servings.**

*Look for this brand of mashed potatoes in the meat department of your grocery store.

Carrot-Apricot Mash

This vivid apricot-kissed side dish is chock-full of vitamins.

Prep: 15 min.   Cook: 20 min.

2   lb. carrots, peeled and sliced
½   cup apricot nectar
1   cup chicken broth
2   garlic cloves, sliced
3   Tbsp. grated orange rind
¼   cup butter
3   Tbsp. whipping cream
½   tsp. salt

Combine first 5 ingredients in a large saucepan; bring to a boil. Cover, reduce heat, and simmer 15 to 20 minutes or until carrots are very tender.

Process carrot mixture, in batches, in a food processor until smooth, stopping to scrape down sides as needed. Return mixture to saucepan; add butter, whipping cream, and salt. Cook over medium heat, stirring constantly, until warm. **Yield: 6 to 8 servings.**

quick & easy
Christmas Creamed Corn

Bet you never thought frozen corn could end up on your holiday table tasting this good.

Prep: 10 min.   Cook: 15 min.

¼   cup butter
1   medium onion, diced
1   red bell pepper, diced
2   garlic cloves, minced
3   (10-oz.) packages frozen whole kernel corn, thawed
¾   cup heavy whipping cream
1   tsp. sugar
¾   tsp. salt
¼   tsp. pepper

Melt butter in a large nonstick skillet over medium heat. Add onion, bell pepper, and garlic; sauté 8 minutes or until tender.

Process 1 package of corn and ½ cup cream in a blender or food processor until smooth. Add puree, remaining ¼ cup cream, and remaining corn to skillet. Stir in sugar, salt, and pepper. Cook, stirring often, 5 minutes, or until heated and most of liquid evaporates. **Yield: 6 to 8 servings.**

make ahead
Butternut Squash Casserole with Pecan Streusel

As an option, you can use canned pumpkin puree or yams
instead of the squash in this recipe.

Prep: 15 min.   Cook: 40 min.   Other: 5 min.

3   (12-oz.) packages frozen cooked butternut squash,
      thawed (we tested with McKenzie)
1   cup firmly packed light brown sugar
½   cup half-and-half
¼   cup butter, melted
2   large eggs, lightly beaten
½   tsp. salt
½   tsp. ground cinnamon
¼   tsp. ground allspice
¼   tsp. ground cloves
1   tsp. vanilla extract
¼   cup all-purpose flour
¼   cup firmly packed light brown sugar
3   Tbsp. cold butter, cut into pieces
½   cup chopped pecans

Combine first 10 ingredients in a large bowl; stir well.
Place in a lightly greased 11" x 7" baking dish.
Combine flour and ¼ cup brown sugar. Cut in 3 Tbsp.
butter with a pastry blender until crumbly. Stir in nuts.
Sprinkle over squash. Bake, uncovered, at 375° for 40
minutes or until edges are lightly browned. Let casserole
stand 5 minutes before serving. **Yield: 8 to 10 servings.**

Apple-Raisin Dressing

If you're a fan of moist dressing, use the larger amount of broth.

Prep: 16 min.   Cook: 1 hr., 14 min.

¼   cup butter
1   large onion, diced
2   celery ribs, diced (about 1 cup)
2   Granny Smith apples, diced (about 3 cups)
2   tsp. rubbed sage
½   tsp. salt
¼   tsp. freshly ground black pepper
1   (16-oz.) package herb-seasoned stuffing mix
      (we tested with Pepperidge Farm)
1   cup golden raisins
1   cup chopped pecans, toasted
2½   to 3 cups chicken broth
2   large eggs, lightly beaten

Melt butter in a large skillet over medium-high heat.
Add onion and celery, and sauté 10 minutes or until tender. Add apple; sauté 3 minutes or until tender. Stir in
sage, salt, and pepper.
Combine sautéed mixture, stuffing, raisins, and pecans
in a large bowl. Add chicken broth and eggs; stir well.
Spoon dressing into a lightly greased 13" x 9" baking
dish. Bake, uncovered, at 325° for 50 to 60 minutes or
until well browned. **Yield: 10 to 12 servings.**

editor's favorite
Crumb-Topped Spinach Casserole

This quick, cheesy side, with its crunchy herbed topping,
can be ready to bake in just over the time it takes to preheat
the oven.

Prep: 13 min.   Cook: 43 min.

2   Tbsp. butter
1   medium onion, diced
2   garlic cloves, minced
4   (10-oz.) packages frozen chopped spinach, thawed
½   (8-oz.) package cream cheese, softened
2   Tbsp. all-purpose flour
2   large eggs
½   tsp. salt
¼   tsp. pepper
1   cup milk
1   (8-oz.) package shredded Cheddar cheese
1   cup Italian-seasoned Japanese breadcrumbs
      (panko) or homemade breadcrumbs
3   Tbsp. butter, melted

Melt 2 Tbsp. butter in a large nonstick skillet over
medium heat. Add onion and garlic, and sauté 8 minutes
or until tender.
Meanwhile, drain spinach well, pressing between paper
towels to remove excess moisture.
Blend cream cheese and flour in a large bowl until
smooth. Whisk in eggs, salt, and pepper. Gradually whisk
in milk until blended. Add sautéed onions, spinach, and
cheese, stirring to blend. Spoon into a lightly greased
11" x 7" baking dish.
Combine breadcrumbs and 3 Tbsp. melted butter in a
small bowl; toss well, and sprinkle over casserole.
Bake, uncovered, at 350° for 30 to 35 minutes or until
thoroughly heated and breadcrumbs are browned. **Yield:
8 to 10 servings.**

Broccoli with Caramelized Garlic and Pine Nuts

Buy bagged broccoli florets for convenience.

Prep: 5 min. Cook: 16 min.

⅓   cup pine nuts
¼   cup butter
1   Tbsp. olive oil
6   garlic cloves, thinly sliced
1   lb. broccoli florets
½   tsp. salt
⅛   tsp. dried crushed red pepper

Toast pine nuts in a large skillet over medium heat 6 minutes or until lightly browned. Remove from skillet, and set aside.

Heat butter and oil in same skillet over medium heat until butter melts. Add garlic, and sauté 1 to 2 minutes or until lightly browned. Add broccoli, salt, and crushed red pepper. Sauté 8 minutes or until broccoli is tender. Stir in pine nuts before serving. **Yield: 6 servings.**

Green Beans with Toasted Almonds and Lemon

If your grocer doesn't carry bags of pretrimmed green beans, start with 1¾ lb. of untrimmed beans to get an equivalent amount of beans called for here.

Prep: 10 min. Cook: 15 min.

2   (12-oz.) packages trimmed fresh green beans
2   Tbsp. olive oil
2   large garlic cloves, minced
2   tsp. grated lemon rind
½   tsp. salt
¼   tsp. pepper
3   Tbsp. fresh lemon juice
⅓   cup sliced almonds, toasted

Cook green beans in boiling salted water to cover 5 to 7 minutes or until crisp-tender; drain. Plunge beans into a bowl of ice water to stop the cooking process; drain.

Heat oil in a large skillet over medium heat; add garlic, and sauté 1 minute or until golden. Stir in green beans, lemon rind, salt, and pepper; sauté 4 minutes or until beans are thoroughly heated. Add lemon juice and almonds; toss well. **Yield: 6 to 8 servings.**

Fruit and Nut Rice Pilaf

Prep: 5 min. Cook: 16 min.

2   Tbsp. butter
1   medium onion, diced
2   celery ribs, diced
½   cup chicken broth
1   (7-oz.) package dried fruit bits
2   (8.8-oz.) packages microwave-ready long grain and wild rice (we tested with Uncle Ben's)
1   cup chopped walnuts or pecans, toasted
¼   cup chopped flat-leaf parsley
¼   tsp. pepper

Melt butter in a large skillet over medium heat. Add onion and celery, and sauté 5 minutes or until tender. Add broth and fruit; bring to a boil. Cover; reduce heat, and cook 5 minutes or until fruit is softened. Stir in rice; cook, stirring often, 4 minutes or until rice is heated. Stir in walnuts, parsley, and pepper. **Yield: 6 to 8 servings.**

Sweet Potato Galette

Prep: 15 min. Cook: 33 min.

2   lb. sweet potatoes, peeled and sliced into ⅛"-thick rounds
¼   cup unsalted butter, melted and divided
2   Tbsp. all-purpose flour
1   tsp. salt
½   tsp. pepper
¼   tsp. freshly grated nutmeg

Combine sweet potatoes and 2 Tbsp. butter in a large bowl, tossing to coat. Combine flour and next 3 ingredients; sprinkle over potatoes. Toss potatoes to coat.

Place remaining 2 Tbsp. butter in a 10" cast-iron skillet or other large ovenproof skillet. Arrange 1 layer of sweet potatoes in slightly overlapping concentric circles in skillet. Top with remaining sweet potatoes.

Cut a circle of nonstick aluminum foil; place over potatoes. Place a 9" cast-iron skillet on top of foil to weight the galette. Cook galette over medium heat 5 minutes without disturbing. Transfer weighted skillet to oven; bake at 375° for 10 minutes. Remove top skillet and foil, and bake galette 15 more minutes or until potatoes are tender. Loosen edges of galette with a spatula to prevent sticking. Invert onto serving plate; serve warm. **Yield: 6 servings.**

Broccoli with Caramelized Garlic and Pine Nuts

Fruit and Nut Rice Pilaf

Sweet Potato Galette

HALF-HOUR *Holiday Food*

Easy meal ideas for busy people come together in this collection of casseroles and skillet dinners. Most of the recipes are one-dish wonders, and each bakes in about 30 minutes.

Chicken and Broccoli Cobbler

Leftover turkey or a rotisserie chicken works equally well in this easy casserole dotted with Christmas red and green. Crisp sourdough croutons are its crowning glory. Use bagged broccoli florets from the grocery produce section. There's no need to precook the broccoli—it will be crisp-tender when the casserole is bubbly.

Prep: 16 min.   Cook: 30 min.

¼	cup butter, melted
5	oz. cubed sourdough bread (3 cups)
½	cup refrigerated grated Parmesan cheese
3	cups small broccoli florets
3	cups chopped cooked chicken
½	cup drained chopped roasted red bell pepper
1	(10-oz.) container refrigerated Alfredo sauce
½	cup sour cream
2	Tbsp. dry sherry

Drizzle butter over bread cubes in a large bowl; sprinkle with cheese, and toss well.

Combine broccoli and next 5 ingredients in a large bowl. Spoon filling into a lightly greased 2-qt. rectangular or oval baking dish or individual baking dishes; top with bread cubes.

Bake, uncovered, at 400° for 30 minutes (20 to 25 minutes for individual cobblers) or until bubbly and top is toasted. **Yield: 4 servings.**

Chicken and Rice Casserole

To speed things up, use a rotisserie chicken for this family-friendly casserole.

Prep: 20 min.   Cook: 25 min.

2	Tbsp. butter or margarine
1	medium onion, finely chopped
3	cups chopped cooked chicken
1½	cups frozen petite peas
1½	cups (6 oz.) shredded sharp Cheddar cheese
1	cup mayonnaise
1	(10¾-oz.) can cream of chicken soup
1	(8.8-oz.) package microwaveable rice of choice (we tested with Uncle Ben's)
1	(8-oz.) can sliced water chestnuts, drained
1	(4-oz.) jar pimientos, drained
3	cups coarsely crushed ridged potato chips (we tested with Ruffles)

Melt butter in a skillet over medium heat. Add onion, and sauté until tender, about 5 minutes. Combine onion, chicken, and next 7 ingredients in a large bowl; toss gently. Spoon mixture into a lightly greased 13" x 9" baking dish. Top with coarsely crushed chips. Bake, uncovered, at 350° for 20 to 25 minutes or until bubbly. **Yield: 8 servings.**

Spanish Chicken, Lemon, and Potatoes

Flavors of the Mediterranean make this juicy chicken a pleasant departure from expected holiday fare.

Prep: 5 min.   Cook: 28 min.

3 Tbsp. extra virgin olive oil
6 skinned and boned chicken thighs
¼ tsp. salt
¼ tsp. freshly ground pepper
1 (20-oz.) package refrigerated red potato wedges
4 large garlic cloves, sliced
2 oz. cured chorizo sausage, diced
½ cup pitted Spanish olives
1 cup chicken broth
1 Tbsp. Hungarian sweet paprika
1 lemon, thinly sliced and seeded

Heat olive oil in a large skillet over medium-high heat. Sprinkle chicken thighs evenly with salt and pepper; add to skillet. Cook 5 minutes or until browned on all sides.

Meanwhile, combine potatoes and next 5 ingredients in a large bowl; toss to coat. Add potato mixture with broth to skillet; top with lemon slices. Cover and cook 20 minutes or until potatoes are tender. **Yield: 6 servings.**

Holiday Shepherd's Pie

Fix this clever casserole whenever you're in the mood for the flavors of Christmas dinner. Substitute your leftover cornbread dressing for the cornbread to pump up the flavor.

Prep: 9 min.   Cook: 26 min.

3 Tbsp. butter, divided
3 cups prechopped fresh onion, bell pepper, and celery blend
2 cups coarsely crumbled day-old (savory not sweet) cornbread
3 cups chopped cooked turkey
1 cup turkey gravy (we tested with Heinz)
½ tsp. salt
½ tsp. freshly ground black pepper
1 (1.5 lb.) package refrigerated mashed potatoes (we tested with Simply Potatoes)
1 cup whole-berry cranberry sauce

Melt 2 Tbsp. butter in a large skillet over medium-high heat; add onion, bell pepper, and celery blend, and sauté

8 minutes or until tender. Combine sautéed vegetables, cornbread, turkey, and next 3 ingredients in a large bowl. Toss gently. Spoon mixture into a lightly greased 11" x 7" baking dish. Cover to keep warm.

Meanwhile, heat potatoes in microwave according to package directions. Stir in remaining 1 Tbsp. butter. Spread 1 cup cranberry sauce over turkey mixture. Top with potatoes. Bake, uncovered, at 375° for 15 minutes or until thoroughly heated. **Yield: 6 servings.**

editor's favorite
Poppy Seed Turkey Casserole

Turkey puts a new spin on this classic cracker-topped casserole. Add some broccoli florets to introduce color and a veggie.

Prep: 12 min.   Cook: 25 min.

3 to 4 cups chopped cooked turkey
1 (10¾-oz.) can cream of chicken and mushroom soup
1 (16-oz.) container sour cream or light sour cream
1½ cups (6 oz.) shredded sharp Cheddar cheese
3 Tbsp. poppy seeds
1 sleeve of whole wheat round buttery crackers (we tested with Ritz), crushed*
¼ cup butter or margarine, melted

Combine first 5 ingredients in a large bowl; stir well. Spoon into a lightly greased 11" x 7" baking dish. Top with crushed crackers. Drizzle with melted butter. Bake, uncovered, at 350° for 25 to 30 minutes or until bubbly. Let stand 10 minutes before serving. **Yield: 6 servings.**

*You can crush the crackers while they're still in the sleeve; then open at one end, and sprinkle over casserole.

Chopped Cooked Chicken
Recipes on the previous page, this page, and pages 112 and 114 that call for chopped cooked chicken can make use of a rotisserie chicken. It's easiest to pull the meat off the carcass as soon as you get in from the grocery, while the chicken is still warm. Shred or chop chicken, seal it in a zip-top bag, and chill it until ready to use. You can also freeze it up to a month.

Ranch Turkey Ravioli Casserole

This fun twist on lasagna uses ravioli.

Prep: 18 min.   Cook: 28 min.   Other: 15 min.

1   (15-oz.) can black beans, rinsed and drained
1   (14.5-oz.) can petite diced tomatoes, drained
½   cup chopped fresh cilantro
1   tsp. ground cumin
2   cups green enchilada sauce (we tested with
     La Preferida)
2   (9-oz.) packages refrigerated cheese ravioli
2   cups chopped cooked turkey
½   cup sliced green onions
1   cup (4 oz.) shredded Mexican four-cheese blend

Combine first 4 ingredients in a bowl.

Spread ½ cup enchilada sauce in a lightly greased
11" x 7" baking dish. Arrange half of ravioli over sauce.
Top with half of black bean mixture, 1 cup turkey, ¼ cup
green onions, and ½ cup enchilada sauce. Repeat layers.
Pour remaining sauce over top; sprinkle with cheese.

Bake, uncovered, at 400° for 28 minutes or until
thoroughly heated and lightly browned. Let stand
15 minutes before serving. **Yield: 6 servings.**

quick & easy
Quick Skillet Rigatoni

Prep: 4 min.   Cook: 15 min.

8   oz. uncooked rigatoni
1   Tbsp. olive oil
1   medium onion, finely chopped
½   lb. ground round
1   (8-oz.) package sliced fresh mushrooms
2   tsp. chopped fresh rosemary
½   cup dry white wine or chicken or beef broth
1   (15-oz.) can seasoned tomato sauce for lasagna
     (we tested with Hunt's)
Grated Parmesan cheese
Freshly ground pepper

Cook rigatoni according to package directions; drain
and keep warm.

While pasta cooks, heat oil in a large skillet over
medium-high heat. Add onion, ground round, mushrooms,
and rosemary. Cook 8 minutes or until meat crumbles
and is no longer pink. Add wine; bring to a boil. Cook

2 minutes or until almost all liquid evaporates. Stir in
cooked pasta and tomato sauce; cover and simmer 3 minutes or until thoroughly heated. Sprinkle each serving
with grated Parmesan cheese and pepper. **Yield: 4 servings.**

make ahead
Chili Mini Lasagna

*Baking this lasagna in two loaf pans makes for easy transport
to holiday get-togethers, covered-dish parties, or to a friend in
need. We discovered these oven-ready noodles fit perfectly
in loaf pans. Use disposable aluminum pans for no-fuss
cleanup.*

Prep: 16 min.   Cook: 34 min.   Other: 8 hr., 10 min.

1   lb. ground round
1   Tbsp. chili powder
1   (15-oz.) can white kidney beans, rinsed and
     drained
1   large egg, lightly beaten
1   (15-oz.) container ricotta cheese
3¼ cups roasted tomato salsa (we tested with Ariba)
6   oven-ready lasagna noodles
3   cups (12 oz.) shredded Cheddar-Jack cheese
Sour cream (optional)

Cook ground beef in a large skillet over medium heat,
stirring until meat crumbles and is no longer pink; drain
and return to pan. Stir in chili powder and **kidney** beans.

Combine egg and ricotta in a small bowl; set aside.

Spread 2 tablespoons salsa in each of 2 lightly greased
9" x 5" loaf pans. Arrange 1 noodle over salsa in each
pan. Spoon one-fourth ricotta mixture and one-fourth
chili mixture over noodle in each pan; sprinkle each with
½ cup cheese. Spread ½ cup salsa over cheese in each
pan. Repeat layers. Top each pan with another noodle,
1 cup salsa, covering noodle layer completely in each
pan. Sprinkle each lasagna with remaining cheese. Cover
tightly with aluminum foil, and refrigerate overnight.
Bring to room temperature before baking.

Bake, covered, at 400° for 25 minutes; uncover and
bake 5 more minutes or until lightly browned and bubbly.
Let stand 10 minutes before serving. Serve with sour
cream, if desired. **Yield: 2 lasagnas/ 8 servings.**

Pasta and Greens Torte

Pasta and Greens Torte

A well-seasoned cast-iron skillet is in order for this impressive deep-dish entrée.

Prep: 12 min.   Cook: 28 min.   Other: 10 min.

1   lb. fresh Swiss chard*
8   large eggs
1   cup milk
1   cup ricotta cheese
1½   tsp. dried thyme
1½   tsp. salt
½   tsp. pepper
1   (9-oz.) package refrigerated linguine, cut in half
3   Tbsp. olive oil
2   cups (8 oz.) shredded Italian blend cheese

Bring 4 qt. water to a boil in a 6-qt. Dutch oven.

While water comes to a boil, remove and discard stems and ribs from chard. Coarsely chop leaves. Wash chard thoroughly in cold water; drain well. Process eggs and next 5 ingredients in a blender until smooth.

Add chard leaves and pasta to boiling water. Return water to a boil; boil 1 minute. Drain well, pressing out excess moisture from chard with the back of a spoon. Return pasta and greens to pan; toss until blended.

Brush a 10" cast-iron skillet with olive oil. Arrange pasta and greens in skillet; sprinkle with cheese. Pour egg mixture over cheese, pressing to submerge pasta and greens in liquid.

Place skillet over medium heat for 2 minutes. Immediately transfer to hot oven. Bake at 400° for 25 minutes or until golden and set. Let stand 10 minutes before inverting onto a serving platter, if desired, and cutting into wedges. **Yield: 6 to 8 servings.**

*It's easier to prepare greens if you chop or tear them first before cleaning in several washings of cold water. Drain well between washings, and finish with a whirl in a salad spinner to remove sandy grit.

editor's favorite
Southwestern Egg Casserole

This dish is great for brunch or Sunday night supper. It's spicy—for a milder flavor, choose plain Monterey Jack cheese.

Prep: 27 min.   Cook: 30 min.

1   lb. mild ground pork sausage
1   small onion, chopped
½   green bell pepper, chopped
2   (10-oz.) cans diced tomatoes and green chiles, undrained
8   (10") flour tortillas, torn into bite-size pieces
3   cups (12 oz.) shredded Monterey Jack cheese with peppers or Monterey Jack cheese
6   large eggs
2   cups milk
1   tsp. salt
½   tsp. pepper
¼   cup chopped fresh cilantro

Cook sausage in a large skillet over medium-high heat, stirring until it crumbles and is no longer pink. Drain and return to skillet. Add chopped onion and bell pepper to sausage; sauté over medium heat 5 minutes or until vegetables are tender. Stir in tomatoes and green chiles; reduce heat. Cover and simmer 10 minutes.

Layer half each of tortilla pieces, sausage mixture, and cheese in a lightly greased 13" x 9" baking dish. Repeat layers.

Whisk together eggs and next 3 ingredients; pour over layers in dish.

Bake, uncovered, at 350° for 25 to 30 minutes or until lightly browned and set in center. Sprinkle with cilantro before serving. **Yield: 8 servings.**

SCRUMPTIOUS GOODIES FROM THE KITCHEN AND HANDMADE GIFT
WRAPPINGS CONVEY SWEET GREETINGS TO EVERYONE ON YOUR LIST.

Giving

GIFTS FROM THE *Kitchen*

Mix, bake, wrap, and deliver some really delectable goodies this holiday season. These easy recipes and pretty packaging ideas will inspire you to start today.

gift idea • make ahead

Chocolate-Drenched Chipotle-Roasted Nuts

These spicy-sweet nuts slathered in chocolate are sure to go fast—serve them as a fun pickup dessert, or wrap them in cellophane bags to give as gifts.

Prep: 5 min.   Cook: 1 hr., 4 min.

3	Tbsp. sugar
2	Tbsp. water
2	tsp. minced chipotle pepper in adobo sauce
½	tsp. salt
2	Tbsp. butter, melted
1	cup pecan halves
1	cup walnut halves
½	cup semisweet chocolate morsels
1	Tbsp. shortening
¼	cup white chocolate morsels, melted

Combine first 4 ingredients in a medium-size nonstick skillet. Cook over medium heat until mixture comes to a boil. Remove from heat; stir in butter. Add nuts, and gently stir to coat. Spoon coated nuts in a single layer onto a rimmed baking sheet lined with parchment paper.

Bake at 250° for 1 hour, stirring every 15 minutes. Spread nuts on wax paper or parchment paper to cool, breaking apart large clumps as nuts cool.

Melt semisweet chocolate morsels and shortening in a small saucepan over low heat, stirring until smooth. Remove from heat; cool slightly. Toss cooled nuts in semisweet chocolate until well coated. Return nuts to wax paper, and let harden. Drizzle white chocolate over nuts (do not toss). Let harden. **Yield: 3 cups.**

Tip: Speed up the chocolate hardening process by popping the jelly-roll pan into the freezer for 5 to 10 minutes.

A drizzling of white chocolate makes these spicy chocolate nuts even more decadent.

editor's favorite • gift idea • make ahead

Chile-Spiced Sugared Nuts

Prep: 9 min.   Cook: 30 min.

2	large egg whites
1	Tbsp. water
1⅔	cups (½ lb.) pecan halves
1⅔	cups (½ lb.) whole natural almonds
1½	cups sugar
2	Tbsp. ground cinnamon
2	tsp. salt
1½	tsp. chipotle chile powder or other chile powder

Beat egg whites and water in a bowl until blended. Add nuts to egg whites, stirring to coat; drain in a colander.

Combine sugar and next 3 ingredients in another bowl. Add nuts, in batches, to spiced sugar, shaking bowl to coat nuts. Transfer nuts with a slotted spoon to a large rimmed baking sheet lined with parchment paper, spreading nuts into a single layer.

Bake at 300° for 30 minutes or until coating is crisp, stirring after 25 minutes. Cool completely. Break big clusters apart. Store in airtight containers. **Yield: about 6 cups.**

Prize-Winning Barbecue Rub

Backyard chefs will go for this spicy-sweet homemade rub, which is worthy of prizewinning status once it hits food on the grill. Package it in sprinkle-top jars for giving. (pictured on page 157)

Prep: 6 min.

¾ cup firmly packed light brown sugar
½ cup paprika
2½ Tbsp. coarse sea salt
1½ Tbsp. ground black pepper
1 Tbsp. garlic powder
1 Tbsp. onion powder
2 tsp. ground ginger
1 tsp. ground cumin
½ tsp. ground red pepper

Combine all ingredients in a small bowl, stirring well. Store in an airtight container at room temperature. Sprinkle rub evenly over meat, poultry, or fish. Rub in seasonings with fingers. Grill as desired. **Yield: 2 cups.**

Grilled Ribs: Rub ¾ cup Prize-Winning Barbecue Rub evenly onto 4 pounds pork spareribs in a shallow roasting pan; cover with aluminum foil, and refrigerate overnight. Bake ribs, covered, at 300° for 3 hours. Drain excess liquid. Brush ribs with some of 1½ cups favorite barbecue sauce (we tested with Sticky Fingers) blended with 1 Tbsp. Prize-Winning Barbecue Rub. Grill ribs, covered, over medium heat (300° to 350°) for 15 to 20 minutes, basting heavily with rest of sauce. **Yield: 4 to 6 servings.**

Cedar-Planked Barbecue Salmon: Soak 1 cedar plank in water overnight; drain. Place a 2-pound salmon fillet, skin side down, on soaked plank. Sprinkle 2 Tbsp. Prize-Winning Barbecue Rub evenly over flesh side of salmon. Grill, covered with grill lid, over medium-high heat (350° to 400°) for 25 minutes or until salmon flakes with a fork. **Yield: 4 servings.**

Holiday Inspiration

The secret to transforming food into a great gift is all in the presentation. Look for unique tins, festive cellophane bags, decorative tissue, or to-go cartons for packaging. Then add your special touch: a ribbon, a homemade gift tag, and a Christmas keepsake such as a spreader or tiny spoon.

Stone-Ground Cornmeal-Pecan Shortbread

These savory rounds are like cheese straws—only better, thanks to the texture that cornmeal adds.

Prep: 30 min.   Cook 17 min. per batch

14 Tbsp. butter, softened
1 (8-oz.) wedge Parmesan cheese, finely shredded
1 tsp. salt
¼ tsp. ground red pepper
½ cup stone-ground yellow cornmeal
½ cup finely chopped pecans
1½ cups all-purpose flour

Place first 4 ingredients in a mixing bowl; beat at medium speed with an electric mixer 2 minutes or until well blended. Add cornmeal and chopped pecans, beating just until blended. Gradually add flour, beating at low speed until blended. (Dough will be crumbly, yet moist enough to cling together when pressed.)

Roll out dough ¼" thick on a sheet of parchment paper. Cut out dough using a 2" round cookie cutter, and place rounds 1" apart on parchment paper-lined large baking sheets.

Bake at 350° for 15 to 17 minutes or until lightly browned and crisp. Remove shortbread from baking sheets, and cool completely on a wire rack. Re-roll scraps of dough ¼" thick, cut out, and bake as above. **Yield: 3½ dozen.**

Saga Blue and Walnut Spread

Prep: 4 min.

1 (8-oz.) package cream cheese, softened
1 (5-oz.) package Saga or other favorite blue cheese, rind trimmed
½ cup chopped walnuts, toasted
2 tsp. fresh lemon juice
⅛ tsp. ground red pepper
Specialty crackers
Celery sticks

Beat cream cheese and blue cheese at medium speed with an electric mixer until smooth. Stir in walnuts, lemon juice, and pepper. Serve with crackers or celery sticks. Store in refrigerator. Bring to room temperature before serving. **Yield: 1½ cups.**

editor's favorite • gift idea • make ahead
Savory Cheese Truffles with Chives
Prep: 19 min. Other: 3 hr.

Truffles turn savory in these bite-size cheese balls. Pack all three flavor variations in small tins or other decorative containers to share with friends. For a special gift, add a bottle of crisp, dry white wine. These "personal cheese balls" make a great appetizer served with crackers.

1	(8-oz.) package cream cheese, softened
6	oz. goat cheese
1	tsp. fresh lemon juice
2	Tbsp. minced fresh chives
2	tsp. jarred roasted minced garlic
½	tsp. cracked black pepper
1	cup finely chopped pecans, toasted
½	cup chopped flat-leaf parsley

Beat first 3 ingredients at medium speed with an electric mixer until smooth. Stir in chives, garlic, and pepper. Cover and chill at least 2 hours or until firm.

Shape cheese mixture into 1" balls. Roll cheese balls in pecans and parsley. Cover and chill at least 1 hour. **Yield: 2 dozen.**

Curried Truffles: Beat cream cheese, goat cheese, and 2 tsp. curry powder at medium speed with an electric mixer until smooth (omitting lemon juice, chives, garlic, pepper, pecans, and parsley). Stir in 1 Tbsp. finely chopped green onion, 2 tsp. mango chutney, and ¼ teaspoon salt. Cover and chill at least 2 hours or until firm.

Combine ½ cup finely chopped dried cranberries, ½ cup finely chopped dried apricots, and ½ cup finely chopped toasted almonds. Shape cheese mixture into 1" balls. Roll cheese balls in dried fruit mixture. Cover and chill at least 1 hour. **Yield: 2 dozen.**

Honey Mustard Truffles: Beat cream cheese, goat cheese, and 2 Tbsp. honey mustard at medium speed with an electric mixer until smooth (omitting lemon juice, chives, garlic, pepper, pecans, and ½ cup parsley). Stir in 1 Tbsp. chopped flat-leaf parsley and ¼ tsp. ground red pepper. Cover and chill at least 2 hours or until firm.

Shape cheese mixture into 1" balls. Roll cheese balls in 1 cup finely chopped honey-roasted peanuts. Cover and chill at least 1 hour. **Yield: 2 dozen.**

Stone-Ground Cornmeal-Pecan Shortbread

Curried Truffles,
Savory Cheese Truffles with Chives

Mini Pumpkin Spice Loaves

Honey-Baked Chunky Granola

Baskets & Jars
Collect baskets and various sizes of new and vintage jars in a Christmas storage tub. When it's time to plan holiday food gifts, you'll have a head start.

ultimate Fudge Sauce

Candy Slabs

Peppermint-White Chocolate Candy Slabs

Prep: 9 min.   Cook: 1½ min.   Other: 1 hr.

24	round red and green hard peppermint candies
2	(12-oz.) packages white chocolate morsels
1	tsp. peppermint extract

Line 3 (9" x 5") loaf pans with multipurpose sealing wrap (we tested with Press 'N Seal); set aside. (Use disposable loaf pans from the grocery store, if desired.)

Place candies in a zip-top plastic freezer bag. Coarsely crush candies using a meat mallet or rolling pin. Set aside crushed candies, reserving 3 Tbsp. separately for topping.

Microwave white chocolate morsels in a large microwave-safe bowl at 70% power for 1 minute and 15 seconds. (Morsels will not look melted.) Stir morsels until melted. Microwave again 15-second intervals, if necessary.

Add peppermint extract and larger portion of crushed candies to melted chocolate, stirring until evenly distributed.

Quickly spread melted white chocolate evenly in prepared pans; sprinkle with reserved 3 Tbsp. candies, pressing gently with fingertips. Let stand 1 hour or until firm. **Yield: 3 slabs/about 1¾ lb.**

Peanut Brittle Candy Slabs: Melt white chocolate as directed in recipe above, gently folding in 1½ cups crushed storebought peanut brittle and ½ cup creamy peanut butter; spread evenly in prepared loaf pans. Dollop 1 Tbsp. creamy peanut butter over candy mixture in each loaf pan; swirl with a knife. Sprinkle ½ cup crushed peanut brittle evenly over candy in pans, pressing gently with fingertips. **Yield: 3 slabs/2⅓ lb.**

Hello Dolly Candy Slabs: Measure and combine ⅔ cup each miniature semisweet chocolate morsels, toasted flaked coconut, chopped pecans, and chopped graham crackers; set aside ½ cup of this mix for topping. Melt white chocolate as directed in recipe above, gently folding in combined ingredients; spread evenly in prepared loaf pans. Sprinkle reserved ½ cup topping mixture over candy in pans, pressing gently with fingertips. **Yield: 3 slabs/2 lb.**

Mini Pumpkin Spice Loaves

Prep: 12 min.   Cook: 45 min.   Other: 10 min.

¾	cup unsalted butter, softened
3	cups sugar
3	large eggs
3	cups all-purpose flour
2	tsp. baking powder
1	tsp. baking soda
½	tsp. salt
1	tsp. ground cinnamon
1	tsp. ground cloves
¼	tsp. ground nutmeg
1	cup chopped pecans, toasted
¾	cup golden raisins
2	cups canned pumpkin
1	tsp. vanilla extract
	Cream Cheese Icing

Beat butter at medium speed with an electric mixer until creamy. Gradually add sugar, beating well. Add eggs, 1 at a time, beating just until yellow disappears.

Combine flour and next 6 ingredients in a medium bowl. Add pecans and raisins, tossing to coat. Add flour mixture to butter mixture alternately with pumpkin, beginning and ending with flour mixture. Stir in vanilla.

Spoon batter into 12 greased and floured 5" x 3" mini loaf pans. (We tested with Anolon nonstick 6-cavity mini loaf pans, filling each cup ⅔ full.) Bake at 325° for 45 minutes or until a wooden pick inserted in center comes out clean. Cool in pans on a wire rack 10 minutes, remove from pans, and let cool completely. Frost loaves with Cream Cheese Icing. **Yield: 12 loaves.**

Cream Cheese Icing:

Prep: 4 min.

1	(3-oz.) package cream cheese, softened
3	Tbsp. unsalted butter, softened
½	tsp. vanilla extract
2¾	cups powdered sugar
2	Tbsp. milk

Beat first 3 ingredients at medium speed with an electric mixer until creamy; gradually add powdered sugar, beating until smooth. Add milk, 1 Tbsp. at a time, beating until spreading consistency. (This icing's thick.) **Yield: 1¾ cups.**

gift idea • make ahead • quick & easy

White Chocolate Cookies 'n' Cream Fudge

Beloved chocolate sandwich cookies stud a vanilla fudge landscape.

Prep: 7 min.   Cook: 13 min.   Other: 2 hr.

1   cup sugar
¾   cup butter
1   (5-oz.) can evaporated milk
2   (12-oz.) packages white chocolate morsels
1   (7-oz.) jar marshmallow cream
3   cups coarsely crushed cream-filled chocolate
       sandwich cookies (about 25 cookies), divided
Pinch of salt

Line a greased 9" square pan with aluminum foil; set aside.

Combine first 3 ingredients in a medium saucepan. Cook over medium-high heat, stirring constantly, until mixture comes to a boil; cook 3 minutes, stirring constantly. Remove from heat; add white chocolate morsels, marshmallow cream, 2 cups crushed cookies, and salt. Stir until morsels melt.

Pour fudge into prepared pan. Sprinkle remaining 1 cup cookies over fudge, gently pressing cookies into fudge. Cover and chill until firm (about 1 to 2 hours).

Lift uncut fudge in aluminum foil from pan; remove foil, and cut fudge into squares. **Yield: 4 lb.**

White Chocolate
Cookies 'N Cream
Fudge

Ultimate Fudge Sauce

This sauce is rich, thick, and so delicious. It received our highest rating. (pictured on page 162)

Prep: 6 min.   Cook: 5 min.

1   cup heavy whipping cream
¾   cup sugar
8   oz. unsweetened chocolate, finely chopped
⅓   cup corn syrup
¼   cup unsalted butter
1½   tsp. vanilla extract
⅛   tsp. salt

Combine whipping cream and sugar in a heavy saucepan. Place over medium heat, and cook, stirring constantly, until sugar dissolves. Stir in chocolate, corn syrup, and butter. Cook over medium-low heat, stirring occasionally, until chocolate melts and all ingredients are blended. Remove from heat; stir in vanilla and salt. Let cool to room temperature. Transfer sauce to jars with tight-fitting lids. Store in refrigerator. To serve, spoon sauce into a microwave-safe bowl, and microwave at HIGH for 20-second intervals or until pourable. **Yield: 2½ cups.**

Fleur de Sel Caramel Crunch Cups

French sea salt is the perfect finish for these candy cups. This hand-harvested fine salt looks like tiny snowflakes. Reserve it for recipes that highlight its texture and distinctive clean flavor.

Prep: 31 min.   Cook: 9 min.

2   Tbsp. heavy whipping cream
1   (14-oz.) package caramels
1   cup chopped macadamia nuts, toasted
1   cup coarsely crushed thin pretzel sticks (we tested with Rold Gold)
¼   tsp. vanilla extract
1¾   cups bittersweet chocolate morsels
Fleur de sel (French sea salt) or coarse sea salt

Combine heavy cream and caramels in a small microwave-safe bowl; microwave at HIGH 2 to 3 minutes or until caramels are melted, stirring after every minute. Stir in nuts, pretzels, and vanilla. Spoon mixture into 45 (1½") foil petits four cups lightly greased with cooking spray, filling each two-thirds full; cool completely.

Place chocolate morsels in a small microwave-safe bowl, and microwave at HIGH 1 minute or until melted; stir until smooth. Spoon chocolate evenly over caramel in cups; cool slightly. Sprinkle with fleur de sel, and let candy cups set completely. Store candy cups in an airtight container in a cool, dry place. **Yield: 45 candy cups.**

Honey-Baked Chunky Granola

Enjoy this whole grain crunchy snack sprinkled over ice cream, pancakes, or yogurt. (pictured on page 162)

Prep: 13 min.   Cook: 1 hr., 10 min.

½   cup butter
½   cup honey
½   cup firmly packed light brown sugar
¼   tsp. salt
1   Tbsp. grated orange rind
1   Tbsp. ground cinnamon
2   tsp. vanilla extract
4   cups uncooked regular oats
1   cup raw sunflower seeds
½   cup toasted wheat germ
½   cup whole natural almonds
½   cup coarsely chopped walnuts
½   cup flax seeds
Butter-flavored cooking spray
1   cup dried cherries
1   cup dried cranberries or blueberries
1   cup chopped dried apricots
¾   cup dried organic coconut flakes

Combine first 4 ingredients in a small saucepan. Bring to a simmer over medium heat, and cook 5 minutes, stirring occasionally. Remove from heat; stir in orange rind, cinnamon, and vanilla.

While syrup cooks, toss together oats and next 5 ingredients in a large bowl until blended. Pour syrup over oat mixture, and stir until coated. Using hands coated with butter-flavored cooking spray, very firmly press oat mixture into a large lightly greased rimmed baking sheet.

Bake at 275° for 1 hour and 10 minutes or until toasted and browned (do not stir). Let cool completely in pan.

Toss together cherries and next 3 ingredients in large bowl. When granola is cool, break apart into chunks, and gently stir into dried fruit and coconut. Store granola in airtight jars up to 5 days. **Yield: about 10 cups.**

HOLIDAY *Tags & Bags*

*Be earth friendly and family friendly all at once when you enlist family members
to help fashion festive gift bags and tags from recycled shopping bags and last season's
Christmas cards. In addition to unique wrappings, you'll create fond holiday memories
that will last well beyond the season.*

Green Cards

Have fun, save money, and impress everyone on your gift list when you make your own gift tags. Start with blank paper luggage tags, or cut rectangles from sturdy paper and punch a hole in one end. Now, take that stack of last year's Christmas cards that you couldn't bear to toss out, and cut out the pretty pictures and drawings to embellish your creations. Cut out words and phrases, too, or you can use rub-on transfer letters and words. Of course, you can also write a personal greeting. Try a calligraphic pen for the best results. You can find single pens or pen sets in a variety of colors, as well as blank tags, at crafts, discount, and drug stores. Arrange your cutouts on the blank tags, and glue them in place. Use ribbons, raffia, cording, or twine to attach the tags to packages.

Merry Makeovers
Transform paper shopping bags into colorful gift bags by using printed papers, cutouts, and trimmings to create cheery designs. Small scraps of ribbons and leftover strips of wrapping paper are perfect for this project. Arrange the paper cutouts and trims so they cover any print or images on the recycled bags.

Here's How

Decorate beautiful gift bags the easy way. Start by choosing paper shopping bags from your stash (because they're just too cool to throw away, right?). Look for bags in colors that can be dressed up for the holidays. Plain brown bags offer an excellent neutral canvas for traditional color combinations (such as the ones shown facing page and above), and, of course, red, green, white, silver, and gold bags give endless creative options. Black bags are a dramatic background for vivid colors, such as those in the torn-paper star on the bag shown above.

Gather your supplies. You'll need scissors, glue, and double-stick tape; from there, the possibilities are endless. Collect an assortment of printed papers, ribbons, stickers, buttons, and tags. Check out the scrapbooking section of crafts and discount stores for inexpensive add-ons, such as quotes from vellum phrase books, rub-on transfer letters and designs, brads, photo corners, and other embellishments. Glue or tape your design in place, and complete your wrapping by threading ribbon through cuts made with a craft knife at the top of the bag. Tuck in crisp tissue paper to peep out from the opening.

WHERE TO *Find It*

- page 10—**turkey platter, brown transferware bowl:** Mulberry Heights Antiques, Birmingham, AL, (205) 870-1300; **carving set:** Tricia's Treasures, Birmingham, AL, (205) 871-9779; **glass compote:** The Nest, Birmingham, AL, (205) 870-1264; **glasses, candles:** Pottery Barn, (888) 779-5176, www.potterybarn.com
- pages 10–11—**trug place cards:** Smith and Hawken, (800) 940-1170, www.smithandhawken.com
- page 13—**dinnerware (plates):** Blanc d'Ivoire, www.blancdivoire.com
- page 17—**cake pedestal, Merry Christmas linen:** Attic Antiques, Birmingham, AL, (205) 991-6887
- pages 18 and 21—**ticking napkins:** Pottery Barn, (888) 779-5176, www.potterybarn.com; **milk bottles:** Anthropologie, (800) 309-2500, www.anthropologie.com; **orange juice glasses and caddy:** Attic Antiques, Birmingham, AL, (205) 991-6887
- pages 18–19—**wire basket, rag balls:** Attic Antiques, Birmingham, AL, (205) 991-6887; **large basket centerpiece:** Smith and Hawken, (800) 940-1170, www.smithandhawken.com
- page 21—**bread bowl:** The Nest, Birmingham, AL, (205) 870-1264
- page 23—**plates, platter:** Fortunata, (404) 351-1096, www.fortunatainc.com; **antique towel:** Attic Antiques, Birmingham, AL, (205) 991-6887
- page 24—**casserole dish:** Lamb's Ears, Ltd., Birmingham, AL, (205) 969-3138; **glass bowl:** Bromberg's, Birmingham, AL, (800) 633-4616, www.brombergs.com; **platter:** Pottery Barn, (888) 779-5176, www.potterybarn.com; **flatware caddy, flower container:** *Southern Living At HOME®*, www.southernlivingathome.com for ordering information; **table runner, napkins:** Williams-Sonoma, (877) 812-6235, www.williams-sonoma.com;

dinner plates: Chamart, (212) 684-4130, www.chamartlimoges.com
- page 25—**glasses:** Chamart, (212) 684-4130, www.chamartlimoges.com
- page 27—**dinner plates, cups and saucers, glasses:** Chamart, (212) 684-4130, www.chamartlimoges.com
- page 29—**compotes:** Chamart, (212) 684-4130, www.chamartlimoges.com; **antique flatware:** Tricia's Treasures, Birmingham, AL, (205) 871-9779; **tray for fruit:** *Southern Living At HOME®*, www.southernlivingathome.com for ordering information; **napkins:** Williams-Sonoma, (877) 812-6235, www.williams-sonoma.com
- pages 30–31—**flowers, arrangements:** Park Lane Flowers, Birmingham, AL, (205) 879-7115; **red wine glasses:** A'mano, Mountain Brook, AL, (205) 871-9093; **red runner, brown linens:** Pottery Barn, (888) 779-5176, www.potterybarn.com; **plates, china:** Raynaud at Bromberg's, Birmingham, AL, (800) 633-4616, www.brombergs.com
- page 33—**flowers, arrangements:** Park Lane Flowers, Birmingham, AL, (205) 879-7115
- pages 34 and 37—**plates, china:** Raynaud at Bromberg's, Birmingham, AL, (800) 633-4616, www.brombergs.com
- page 38—**containers:** Michaels, (800) 642-4235, www.michaels.com
- page 40—**Cinnabar Footed Server:** *Southern Living At HOME®*, www.southernlivingathome.com for ordering information
- page 41—**container:** Michaels, (800) 642-4235, www.michaels.com
- page 42—**containers:** Hobby Lobby, (800) 888-0321, www.hobbylobby.com; Michaels, (800) 642-4235, www.michaels.com
- page 43—**metal urn:** Dorothy McDaniel's Flower Market, Birmingham, AL, (205) 871-0092, www.dorothymcdaniel.com;

moss balls and table runner: Smith and Hawken, (800) 940-1170, www.smithandhawken.com
- pages 44–45—**containers:** Hobby Lobby, (800) 888-0321, www.hobbylobby.com; Michaels, (800) 642-4235, www.michaels.com
- pages 48–49—**red vases:** Smith and Hawken, (800) 940-1170, www.smithandhawken.com; **bowls, plates, glassware, green candles:** At Home, Homewood, AL, (205) 879-3510
- pages 50–51—**mercury glass candleholders, brown candles:** Pottery Barn, (888) 779-5176, www.potterybarn.com; **twig balls:** Davis Wholesale Florist, Birmingham, AL, (205) 595-2179; **silver tinsel garland:** Hobby Lobby, (800) 888-0321, www.hobbylobby.com
- pages 52–53—**ornaments, covered candy stands:** Seasons of Cannon Falls, (800) 377-3335, www.seasonsofcannonfalls.com; **glass plates:** Annieglass at Table Matters, Birmingham, AL, (205) 879-0125, www.table-matters.com
- pages 54–55—**glass containers, plates, table runner:** Pottery Barn, (888) 779-5176, www.potterybarn.com; **vellum quote book:** Michaels, (800) 642-4235, www.michaels.com
- pages 56–57—**silver chargers, dinnerware, napkins:** Pier 1, (800) 245-4595, www.pier1.com; **place mats:** Lamb's Ears, Ltd., Birmingham, AL, (205) 969-3138; **ornaments, garland:** Smith and Hawken, (800) 940-1170, www.smithandhawken.com; **mercury glass votives:** Pottery Barn, (888) 779-5176, www.potterybarn.com; **Madeline Hurricane, petite glass domes:** *Southern Living At HOME®*, www.southernlivingathome.com for ordering information

- **page 59—light bulb ornaments:** Seasons of Cannon Falls, (800) 377-3335, www.seasonsofcannonfalls.com; **rub-on transfers, stationery:** Michaels, (800) 642-4235, www.michaels.com
- **pages 62–63—wreath, wreath form:** Oak Street Garden Shop, Birmingham, AL, (205) 870-7542, www.oakstreetgardenshop.com
- **page 64—hanging finial vase:** Seasons of Cannon Falls, (800) 377-3335, www.seasonsofcannonfalls.com; **pinecones:** Davis Wholesale Florist, Birmingham, AL, (205) 595-2179
- **page 65—ornaments:** Target, (800) 591-3869, www.target.com; **glass containers, twigs:** HomeGoods, (800) 614-HOME, www.homegoods.com
- **page 70—plate:** Lamb's Ears, Ltd., Birmingham, AL, (205) 969-3138; **wreath:** Dorothy McDaniel's Flower Market, Birmingham, AL, (205) 871-0092, www.dorothymcdaniel.com
- **pages 72–73—ribbon:** The Christmas Tree, Pelham, AL, (205) 988-8090; **pillows:** Pottery Barn, (888) 779-5176, www.potterybarn.com
- **page 74—leaf ornaments:** Smith and Hawken, (800) 940-1170, www.smithandhawken.com
- **page 75—letter:** Ballard Designs, (800) 536-7551, www.ballarddesigns.com; **wreath:** Dorothy McDaniel's Flower Market, Birmingham, AL, (205) 871-0092, www.dorothymcdaniel.com; **chalkboard wreath:** Park Lane Flowers, Birmingham, AL, (205) 879-7115
- **page 76—garland:** Lagniappe Designs, Birmingham, AL, (205) 870-5061; **painting:** Griffith Art Gallery, Pelham, AL, (205) 985-7969, www.GriffithArtGallery.com; **candles:** At Home, Homewood, AL, (205) 879-3510; Pottery Barn, (888) 779-5176, www.potterybarn.com
- **page 77—glass container:** Pottery Barn, (888) 779-5176, www.potterybarn.com; **colored vases:** A'Mano, Mountain Brook, AL, (205) 871-9093

- **page 78—ornament hooks:** Bronner's Christmas Wonderland, (800) 361-6736, www.bronners.com
- **page 79—stockings:** Simplemente Blanco, (617) 734-3669, www.simplementeblanco.com; **garland:** Smith and Hawken, (800) 940-1170, www.smithandhawken.com
- **pages 80–81—bags, crafting materials:** Michaels, (800) 642-4235, www.michaels.com
- **pages 82–83—wreath, ornaments:** Crispina Design Workshop, (413) 637-0075, www.crispina.com
- **pages 84–85—reindeer, trees, candle-holders, garlands, ribbon:** Christmas & Co., Birmingham, AL, (205) 823-6640, www.christmasandco.com
- **pages 86–87—glass containers:** Michaels, (800) 642-4235, www.michaels.com
- **page 89—containers:** Smith and Hawken, (800) 940-1170, www.smithandhawken.com; **vintage pots:** *Southern Living At HOME®*, www.southernlivingathome.com for ordering information
- **pages 90–91—metal pails:** Main St. Supply, (800) 624-8373, www.mainstsupply.com; **letters:** Pottery Barn Kids, (800) 993-4923, www.potterybarnkids.com; **red stars:** Pottery Barn, (888) 779-5176, www.potterybarn.com; **galvanized stars:** Smith and Hawken, (800) 940-1170, www.smithandhawken.com
- **pages 92–93—stockings 1, 2, 4 ,7:** Pottery Barn Kids, (800) 993-4923, www.potterybarnkids.com; **stockings 3, 6:** Sturbridge Yankee Workshop, (800) 343-1144, www.sturbridgeyankee.com; **stocking 5:** Garnet Hill: (800) 870-3513, www.garnethill.com; **large olive jars:** Tricia's Treasures, Birmingham, AL, (205) 871-9779; **small olive jars:** *Southern Living At HOME®*, www.southernlivingathome.com for ordering information
- **pages 96–97—birch pole:** Atmosphere Home Essentials, Birmingham, AL, (205) 324-9687;

bird houses: Smith and Hawken, (800) 940-1170, www.smithandhawken.com
- **pages 100–101—tags, stamps:** Michaels, (800) 642-4235, www.michaels.com
- **page 101—napkins:** Pottery Barn, (888) 779-5176, www.potterybarn.com
- **pages 102–103—frames:** HomeGoods, (800) 614-HOME, www.homegoods.com; **typography alphabet cards:** Pottery Barn, (888) 779-5176, www.potterybarn.com
- **pages 104–105—urns:** Smith and Hawken, (800) 940-1170, www.smithandhawken.com
- **page 108—platter, tray:** dbO Home, dana@dbohome.com
- **page 116—glasses, tray:** Target, (800) 591-3869, www.target.com; **platter:** dbO Home, dana@dbohome.com
- **page 119—fondue pot, forks:** T.J. Maxx, (800) 285-6299, www.tjmaxx.com
- **page 122—platter:** Tribeca at Lamb's Ears, Ltd., Birmingham, AL, (205) 969-3138
- **page 126—white pedestal:** *Southern Living At HOME®*, www.southernlivingathome.com for ordering information
- **page 139—glass pedestal:** Table Matters, Birmingham, AL, (205) 879-0125, www.table-matters.com
- **page 142—white compote:** *Southern Living At HOME®*, www.southernlivingathome.com for ordering information
- **page 150—linen:** Pottery Barn, (888) 779-5176, www.potterybarn.com
- **page 157—spice jars:** World Market, (877) 967-5362, www.worldmarket.com
- **page 161—ceramic egg carton:** Anthropologie, (800) 309-2500, www.anthropologie.com
- **page 162—canister:** *Southern Living At HOME®*, www.southernlivingathome.com for ordering information
- **pages 168–169—crafting supplies:** Scrap Etc., (205) 985-9323, scrapetc.net; Michaels, (800) 642-4235, www.michaels.com

RECIPE *Index*

GENERAL *Index*

Contributors

Editorial Contributors

Margaret Agnew	Susan Huff
Rebecca Boggan	Debby Maugans
Maureen Callahan	Jackie Mills
Melanie J. Clarke	Katie Stoddard
Georgia Downard	Carole Sullivan
Rebekah Flowers	Karen Wilcher
Caroline Grant	Kelley Self Wilton
Kappi Hamilton	Linda Wright

Thanks to the following homeowners

Cynthia Bankston	Janet and Edward Henderson
Ann and Russell Chambliss	Mary and David Hobbs
Kay Clarke	Susan and Don Huff
Margaret and Will Dickey	Sandi and Brent Ponce
Patsy and Alan Dreher	Barbara and Ed Randle
Bobbie Edwards	Sally and Bill Ratliff
Sharon and Roy Gilbert	Leslie and John Simpson
Courtney and Matt Grill	Katie and Tom Stoddard
Kappi and William Hamilton	Pam and Brett Sutton
Carolyn and John Hartman	Linda Wright

Thanks to these Birmingham businesses

Bromberg's	Griffith Art Gallery
Christine's	Lagniappe Designs
Christmas & Co.	Lamb's Ears, Ltd.
The Christmas Tree	Oak Street Garden Shop
Davis Wholesale Flowers	Park Lane Flowers
Dorothy McDaniel's Flower Market	Pottery Barn
	Table Matters
FlowerBuds, Inc.	Tricia's Treasures

PLANNING FOR THE HOLIDAYS IS PART OF THE FUN, SO GRAB A PEN
AND GET ORGANIZED! USE THE BIG PLANNING CALENDARS TO WRITE
IN EVERY HOLIDAY EVENT AND PARTY. FILL IN THE CHARTS WITH
DECORATING IDEAS AND MENU PLANS, AS WELL AS CHRISTMAS
CARD AND GIFT LISTS.

Holiday Planner

NOVEMBER *2008*

Sunday	Monday	Tuesday	Wednesday
2	3	4	5
9	10	11	12
16	17	18	19
23 30	24	25	26

Thursday	Friday	Saturday
		1
6	*7*	*8*
13	*14*	*15*
20	*21*	*22*
Thanksgiving *27*	*28*	*29*

Holiday-Ready Pantry

Be prepared for seasonal cooking and baking by stocking up on these items.

☐ Assorted coffees, teas, hot chocolate, and eggnog
☐ Wine, beer, and soft drinks
☐ White, brown, and powdered sugars
☐ Ground allspice, cinnamon, cloves, ginger, and nutmeg
☐ Baking soda and baking powder
☐ Seasonal fresh herbs
☐ Baking chocolate
☐ Semisweet chocolate morsels
☐ Assorted nuts
☐ Flaked coconut
☐ Sweetened condensed milk and evaporated milk
☐ Whipping cream
☐ Jams, jellies, and preserves
☐ Raisins, cranberries, and other fresh or dried fruits
☐ Canned pumpkin
☐ Frozen/refrigerated bread dough, biscuits, and croissants

Things to do

DECEMBER *2008*

Sunday	Monday	Tuesday	Wednesday
	1	*2*	*3*
7	*8*	*9*	*10*
14	*15*	*16*	*17*
21	*22*	*23*	Christmas Eve *24*
28	*29*	*30*	New Year's Eve *31*

Thursday	Friday	Saturday
4	*5*	*6*
11	*12*	*13*
18	*19*	*20*
Christmas *25*	*26*	*27*

Suggestions for a Simple Christmas

Try these ideas for keeping things easy this holiday season.

- Recycle old Christmas cards as CD jackets for homemade holiday music mixes.
- Use leftover Christmas cards as seasonal thank-you notes.
- Set a disposable table. Scout out holiday paper products at local home-goods stores or supercenters. Find decorative heavy-duty paper plates, napkins, and table coverings. Shore up plates with holiday chargers underneath.
- Get in the habit of unloading clean dishes straight from the dishwasher right onto the table. This way your table is always set and ready for the next meal.
- Have a cook-free Christmas morning. You know the saying, "Life is short. Eat dessert first." Why not apply it to Christmas morning? Let children (big and small) eat Christmas cookies for breakfast with cold milk and orange juice, and you can stay out of the kitchen and enjoy family time.

Things to do

$\mathcal{D}ecorating$ PLANNER

Use these lines to list what you'll need for seasonal decorations all through the house.

Decorative materials needed

from the yard ....
....

from around the house ....
....

from the store ....
....

other ....
....

Holiday decorations

for the table ....
....

for the door ....
....

for the mantel ....
....

for the staircase ....
....

other ....
....

Seasonal Decorating

Decorate earlier and easier with these tips that transcend the seasons.

• For Thanksgiving, place a grapevine garland on the mantel. Put vases filled with dried leaves, berries, and seedpods on each end of the mantel. Arrange small pumpkins and gourds between the vases. After Thanksgiving, trade the harvest look for a Christmas one. Leave the vine garland in place, and switch out the pumpkins and gourds for fruits such as pineapples, apples, pomegranates, and kumquats. Replace the dried materials in the vases with evergreen clippings and stems of holly berries. For a floral display, use amaryllis blooms, hypericum berries, and bells of Ireland.

• Arrange small vases filled with golden mums on a large tray. Surround the vases with votive candles in harvest hues. Fill in with large seed pods and tiny pumpkins. For Christmas, replace the harvest blooms with paperwhites or white freesia. Use red, white, and/or green votive candles. Wind a shimmery ornament or bead garland around the candles and vases.

• An easy seasonal transition can be as simple as changing the colors of your candles from warm gold and persimmon tones to bright reds, silvers, and golds.

Do-It-Yourself Aromatherapy

Here are recipes for two enticing potpourris—one a spicy citrus, the other a woodland forest scent. Either will add a fabulous Christmassy fragrance to your home. Make extra to package and give as gifts.

• **Citrus and Spice Potpourri:** Break cinnamon sticks into 1" pieces. Combine with 4 whole nutmegs and ½ cup each of star anise; cardamom pods; whole allspice berries; and dried orange, grapefruit, or lemon peel. Add 2 or 3 drops of orange essential oil to the mixture. Makes 3 cups.

• **Winter Forest Potpourri:** Mix together 2 cups of pine needles, 1 cup of pine cone scales or small pinecones, ½ cup juniper berries, and ½ cup rose hips. Add 2 or 3 drops of pine essential oil to the mixture. Makes 4 cups.

Menus FOR THE HOLIDAY SEASON

Menus below are based on recipes in the book.

Appetizer Bash

Honey-Roasted Grape Tomato Crostini (page 109)
Pesto Chicken Quesadillas (page 112)
Pimiento Cheese Fondue (page 112) with dippers
Creole Fried Bow-Ties (page 110)
Savory Cheese Truffles with Chives (page 161)
Poinsettia Sipper (page 32)
Wine   Soft drinks

Pasta Night

Parmesan-Peppercorn Snowflakes (page 109)
Rosemary-Lemon Olives (page 109)
Mixed nuts
Baked Three-Cheese Ziti (page 114)
Green salad   Garlic bread
Favorite gelato with Speckled Vanilla-Hazelnut Brittle
(page 127)

Weekend Brunch

Southwestern Egg Casserole (page 155)
Smoky Brown Sugar Bacon (page 20)
Honey-Baked Chunky Granola (page 165)
Fruit Salad with Lemon-Mint Syrup (page 29)
Cacao and Milk Chocolate Scones (page 125)
Coffee   Orange juice

A Chocolate Tasting Party

Chocolate-Drenched Chipotle-Roasted Nuts (page 159)
Dark Chocolate Truffles with Fleur de Sel (page 123)
Deep Dark Fudge with Candied Ginger (page 120)
Chocolate-Chipotle Fondue (page 119) with dippers
Brownie Buttons (page 116)
Fresh fruit and berries
Chocolate Cream Martini (page 116)

Kids' Night

Chicken and Rice Casserole (page 151)
Christmas Creamed Corn (page 146)
Green beans
Big Crunchy Sugar Cookies (page 133)
Ice cream

Six Holiday Dinners

Coffee-Glazed Ham with Red Eye Gravy (page 143)
Fruit and Nut Rice Pilaf (page 148)
Sweet Potato Galette (page 148)
Green Beans with Toasted Almonds and Lemon (page 148)
Herb Buttermilk Biscuits (page 27)
Pumpkin Pie Ice Cream Fantasy (page 37)

———————

Blue Chip Nachos (page 113)
Roast Pork with Sage and Pecan Pesto (page 143)
Butternut Squash Casserole with Pecan Streusel (page 147)
Broccoli with Caramelized Garlic and Pine Nuts (page 148)
Dinner rolls
Whipped Cream Caramel Cake (page 137)

———————

Savory Cheese Truffles with Chives (page 161)
Rack of Lamb with Garlic-Herb Crust (page 144)
Blue Cheese and Black Pepper Potatoes (page 146)
Crumb-Topped Spinach Casserole (page 147)
Roasted tomatoes
Vanilla-Banana-Caramel Flans (page 120)

———————

Rosemary Beef Tenderloin with Balsamic Peppers (page 145)
Blue Cheese and Black Pepper Potatoes (page 146)
Roasted Brussels Sprout Salad (page 14)
Ice cream with Ultimate Fudge Sauce (page 165)

———————

Chicken and Broccoli Cobbler (page 151)
Christmas Creamed Corn (page 146)
Green Beans with Toasted Almonds and Lemon (page 148)
Chocolate Pecan Pie (page 141)

———————

Honey-Roasted Grape Tomato Crostini (page 109)
Grilled Shrimp Caesar (page 114)
Balsamic Peppers (page 145)
Griddled Grits with Cilantro Oil (page 28), recipe halved
Dark Chocolate Truffles with Fleur de Sel (page 123)

Party PLANNER

Make entertaining easy by using this planning chart to coordinate your party menu.

guests	what they're bringing	serving pieces needed
	☐appetizer ☐beverage ☐bread ☐main dish ☐side dish ☐dessert	
	☐appetizer ☐beverage ☐bread ☐main dish ☐side dish ☐dessert	
	☐appetizer ☐beverage ☐bread ☐main dish ☐side dish ☐dessert	
	☐appetizer ☐beverage ☐bread ☐main dish ☐side dish ☐dessert	
	☐appetizer ☐beverage ☐bread ☐main dish ☐side dish ☐dessert	
	☐appetizer ☐beverage ☐bread ☐main dish ☐side dish ☐dessert	
	☐appetizer ☐beverage ☐bread ☐main dish ☐side dish ☐dessert	
	☐appetizer ☐beverage ☐bread ☐main dish ☐side dish ☐dessert	
	☐appetizer ☐beverage ☐bread ☐main dish ☐side dish ☐dessert	
	☐appetizer ☐beverage ☐bread ☐main dish ☐side dish ☐dessert	
	☐appetizer ☐beverage ☐bread ☐main dish ☐side dish ☐dessert	
	☐appetizer ☐beverage ☐bread ☐main dish ☐side dish ☐dessert	
	☐appetizer ☐beverage ☐bread ☐main dish ☐side dish ☐dessert	
	☐appetizer ☐beverage ☐bread ☐main dish ☐side dish ☐dessert	
	☐appetizer ☐beverage ☐bread ☐main dish ☐side dish ☐dessert	
	☐appetizer ☐beverage ☐bread ☐main dish ☐side dish ☐dessert	

Party Guest List

....
....
....
....
....
....
....
....
....
....
....
....
....
....

Pantry List

....
....
....
....
....
....
....
....
....
....

Party To-Do List

....
....
....
....
....
....
....
....
....
....

Christmas Dinner PLANNER

Get a jump start on the big holiday meal by writing your menu, to-do list, and guest list on these pages.

Menu Ideas

....
....
....
....
....
....
....
....

Dinner To-Do List

....
....
....
....
....
....
....
....
....
....
....
....

Christmas Dinner Guest List

....

....

....

....

....

....

....

....

....

....

....

....

Holiday Wine Guide

These tips take the mystery out of serving wine.

• **Decant red wines.** Decanting wine (pouring from one container to another) separates out sediment in older wines and allows young, full-bodied reds the opportunity to "breathe"—releasing flavorful nuances.

• **Select the shape.** A basic white wine glass has a tulip shape. For red wine, the glass has a larger balloon shape. For most wine drinkers, a thin, clear, all-purpose wine glass-either a tulip or balloon shape—with a capacity of 10 to 12 ounces will work. For Champagne, you will want to use a flute; the narrow shape concentrates the wine's bubbles and bouquet and helps maintain its chill. When serving wine, don't fill glasses more than halfway. The remaining space allows for swirling and the development of the wine's bouquet.

• **Serve at the proper temperature.** Most reds are best served between 62° and 65°, so it's okay to stick a bottle in the fridge for 10 or 15 minutes before serving; however, avoid chilling reds for more than 15 minutes. Beaujolais, a smooth, fruity holiday favorite from France, is an exception—it's made to be served slightly chilled (around 58°). Serve white wines between 58° and 62°. Whites that are too cold will taste flat and lifeless. Champagne and sparkling wines are the exception—serve them well-chilled at around 45°. Most refrigerator thermostats are set at around 40°.

• **Save the leftovers.** The key to preserving an opened bottle of wine is to limit its exposure to air. Recorking the wine does not create a tight seal; the wine will not last more than a day or two. The most economical way to preserve an opened bottle is to use a hand-pump vacuum sealer to remove excess air from the bottle. The pump is available in most kitchenware sections of department and grocery stores and allows you to enjoy the wine for an extra two or three days.

Popping the Cork

Though it looks pretty dramatic when it's done in the movies, shooting the cork across the room is not the proper way to open a sparkling wine. Here's how to uncork Champagne and sparkling wine in a more controlled—albeit less showy—fashion.

• Loosen, but don't remove, the cage, keeping your thumb over the top at all times.

• Hold the bottle at a 45° angle. With your thumb over the cork, slowly twist the bottle (not the cork) in one direction while holding the cork firmly.

• Allow the pressure inside the bottle to gently push out the cork.

Gifts AND Greetings

Keep a personalized record of sizes and gifts to use as a ready reference for gift-giving occasions year-round. Write names and addresses on the facing page, and you'll have mailing information close at hand.

Gift List and Size Charts

name /sizes	gift purchased/made	sent/delivered

name ....

jeans_____ shirt_____ sweater_____ jacket_____ shoes_____ belt_____
blouse_____ skirt_____ slacks_____ dress_____ suit_____ coat_____
pajamas_____ robe_____ hat_____ gloves_____ ring_____

name ....

jeans_____ shirt_____ sweater_____ jacket_____ shoes_____ belt_____
blouse_____ skirt_____ slacks_____ dress_____ suit_____ coat_____
pajamas_____ robe_____ hat_____ gloves_____ ring_____

name ....

jeans_____ shirt_____ sweater_____ jacket_____ shoes_____ belt_____
blouse_____ skirt_____ slacks_____ dress_____ suit_____ coat_____
pajamas_____ robe_____ hat_____ gloves_____ ring_____

name ....

jeans_____ shirt_____ sweater_____ jacket_____ shoes_____ belt_____
blouse_____ skirt_____ slacks_____ dress_____ suit_____ coat_____
pajamas_____ robe_____ hat_____ gloves_____ ring_____

name ....

jeans_____ shirt_____ sweater_____ jacket_____ shoes_____ belt_____
blouse_____ skirt_____ slacks_____ dress_____ suit_____ coat_____
pajamas_____ robe_____ hat_____ gloves_____ ring_____

name ....

jeans_____ shirt_____ sweater_____ jacket_____ shoes_____ belt_____
blouse_____ skirt_____ slacks_____ dress_____ suit_____ coat_____
pajamas_____ robe_____ hat_____ gloves_____ ring_____

name ....

jeans_____ shirt_____ sweater_____ jacket_____ shoes_____ belt_____
blouse_____ skirt_____ slacks_____ dress_____ suit_____ coat_____
pajamas_____ robe_____ hat_____ gloves_____ ring_____

Christmas Card List

name	address	sent/delivered

Holiday MEMORIES

Capture highlights of this year's best holiday moments here.

Treasured Traditions

Record your family's favorite holiday customs and pastimes on these lines.

....

....

....

....

....

....

....

....

....

....

....

....

Special Holiday Activities

Keep a list of the seasonal events you look forward to year after year.

....

....

....

....

....

....

....

....

Holiday Visits and Visitors

Keep a list of this year's Christmas visitors. Jot down friend and family news here as well.

....
....
....
....
....
....
....
....
....
....
....
....
....
....
....
....
....
....
....
....
....
....
....

This Year's Favorite Recipes

Appetizers and Beverages ....
....
....
....
....
....

Entrées ....
....
....
....

Sides and Salads ....
....
....
....

Cookies and Candies ....
....
....
....

Desserts ....
....
....
....

Looking AHEAD

Holiday Wrap-up

Use this checklist to keep track of thank-you notes sent for holiday gifts and hospitality.

name	gift and/or event	note sent
		☐
		☐
		☐
		☐
		☐
		☐
		☐
		☐
		☐
		☐
		☐
		☐
		☐

Notes for Next Year

It's never too early to start plans for Christmas 2009!